WHAT WE GO BY

For J and J-R,
B and R

WHAT WE GO BY

RUSSELL HARDIN

Drawings by Rochelle Bonazzi

LATITUDES PRESS

Library of Congress Catalog Card Number: 73—78029.

Latitudes Press Book   # 2
        First Edition, August 1973.
        Second Printing, April 1974.

This book was manufactured in the United States for
Latitudes Press, 297 Garfield Place, Brooklyn, NY 11215,
and simultaneously distributed in cloth and paper editions
by Serendipity Books, 1790 Shattuck, Berkeley, Calif. 94709.

ACKNOWLEDGEMENTS

Seven of these fictions have appeared in Minnesota Review,
Latitudes, Mississippi Review, New Orleans Review and the
anthology *The Sensuous President* (New Rivers Press, 1972).
Thanks due to these editors for permission to reprint.

CONTENTS

I

II

III

I

ON THE KING'S SERVICE

Living in a hotel it takes longer to go to bed, longer to get up, longer to wash, longer to get meals, even longer to go in and out. There are not so many hours in a day as the time it takes longer to do all of a day's things. That is the source of my great perplexity at the moment, for I am on the King's service, and I must live in hotels while travelling through the provinces.

Each day I must see many of the King's subjects and then I must prepare the reports, and yet I have none of the facilities necessary to do any of this. In my hotel rooms there is never a desk. At best there is occasionally—rarely—a small table, at which I can write only by hunching over it until my back refuses to straighten. When there is no table, I must kneel beside my bed until my legs are nearly paralyzed, and in that woeful condition, I am expected to write my reports in a fine script fit to be bound for the archives of the King. There are never chairs, no accommodations for receiving the dozens of subjects from whom I am expected to gather information on the local state of affairs. Almost invariably I must go to them—I! on the King's service must go to them, because the state of my affairs is so dismal that it would be an insult to them, to the King, even to me, to have them come here to my sorry quarters.

The most dreadful moment in my life—when I would almost sooner not continue to live—is the moment of rising in the mornings. It takes a quarter of an hour to put on each stocking, and yet I waste no time—I wonder whether there will be enough time for me to finish dressing before I have to start undressing in time to finish before going back to bed. I cannot understand how it happens that on some days I manage to accomplish some of the King's business between dressing and undressing. And yet when I do not get *all* of the King's business done in the time allotted for my trip, the King has me beaten and, if He is particularly angry, He has me thrown in jail to lament my failure for a while, sometimes for weeks on end.

The cells of the jail are almost the size of my hotel rooms—of the three dimensions of my room at the moment, the longest is vertical, so that I can escape the sensation of being in jail only by lying on my back and looking up; but lying on my back, I am not working; to work therefore is to have the sensation of being in jail.

When I articulate my thoughts, my perplexity only grows deeper. I fall into a cavernous depression. Already I am so far behind that it is hopeless to think of finishing my assignment, and that realization renders my prospects even more thoroughly hopeless.

It has now been three days since I last got out of bed, and the food I bought then is nearly gone, so I must soon rise again. Moreover, tomorrow the maid will come through to change the bed and clean the room—she will not likely treat my obstinance so kindly tomorrow as she did when she found me still in bed yesterday. Perhaps tomorrow I will therefore get up. Then I can set out for the next town.

THE PARTY OVERSEER

Although some of the peasants murmur against our leaders, saying they lead lives of pleasure while we suffer endless and stultifying labor, I would fear for the sanity of our leaders if it were not for their occasional opportunities to relax.

Because the number of issues which come before our leaders is inconceivably vast, and these issues call for the most tedious analysis—a slight change of wording and many an issue requires an altogether different decision—ulcers and nervous prostration are the lot of not a few of our leaders.

Our leaders have the interests of the people at heart. The difficulty of their task cannot be overestimated. The greater burden, I suggest, is not that there are hard and occasionally dramatic decisions of lasting significance to be made; rather, only our leaders can decide which issues call for decisions from them. Hence, they must hear every complaint, every request, every plea.

To hold their parties in the capital where their presence is so conspicuous, where they are so accessible, would hardly encourage undisturbed relaxation for our leaders. Wisely, they come to this remote village. Here they have built a banquet hall beside the small lake where earlier the people of our village used to meet to while away their summer Sunday afternoons. Our leaders are assured a surfeit of fresh fish at their parties in summer months, deer in winter months, and a plentiful variety of fowl in the spring and fall, now that we villagers no longer hunt and fish at the lake. Another value of this location is that foreign dignitaries can be entertained conveniently here. Disturbances have been known to disrupt the capital.

That this village was chosen for their parties was for me a source of great good fortune and honor. Had they (or, actually, an earlier generation of our leaders) chosen another site for their relaxation, naturally the opportunity for me to serve in my present position could not have arisen. But it is a rare man who is qualified to oversee the parties of our leaders. He must be reasonably well schooled; the presence of ignorance at their evenings of diversion would be insulting to our leaders. On the other hand, he cannot be from one of the better families. Their sons increasingly flock to the capital and, perhaps, would equate such work with that of domestic servants. Also, they are ill prepared to go off at a moment's notice to serve for a whole night, indeed, on occasion for nights and days on end with barely a moment's rest. Many times at the end of a full day of hard work in my fields, I have returned to my cottage wishing only to eat and sleep, and have been met at my door by a messenger come to take me to oversee the entertainment of our leaders at a party. Usually I am told that it will last only a short while, but it almost invariably lasts through the night, so that I am too tired to tend my fields the next day, if indeed I am released from our leaders' service before the next day has passed.

I am almost uniquely qualified for my post. Except from the better families, there is hardly a man who is sufficiently educated to oversee our leaders' parties. My father before me, his before him, and so on for generations back, thus served our leaders directly. Long nights of study in my youth, hours of lesson and drill while I worked at his side in the fields, I gratefully accepted from my father. When my mother would try to enter our conversation, he would patiently listen and respond, "Do you wish your son to be ignorant of grammar? One day he will oversee the parties of our leaders." Yet for all his own years of education, for all his years of service to our leaders, when my father retired in his old age he too succumbed to peasant's grammar and, as he had once been loath to converse with my mother, I found it impossible to speak with him.

Our leaders most enjoy parties during the periods of spring and autumn. Each time one of these seasons approaches, I think perhaps it will go better this year and I will have enough time between parties to finish, with my son's help, the work in my fields but, always, when I need only a few days more to finish planting or harvesting, I am called to oversee a party: "It will be only a short evening tonight," the messenger says.

The harvest is inadequate to last the winter and, when I have to beg from my neighbors, they taunt me for my superior grammar—"Ain't got nothin' t' eat, y' say, eh? Well, how d' y' spose that come about?" Were it not so great an honor to serve our leaders, I would find it difficult to attend parties while my family is hungry. Lately, when our leaders are too exhausted to notice, I scrape up enough bits of food to supply my family for a few days. Of course, it would be better to have potatoes and bread—we are unaccustomed to rich desserts and appetizers, and often our stomachs suffer for eating what I am able to bring home.

Occasionally the parties are affairs of state to entertain visiting dignitaries. These are usually the easiest duty. Such parties seldom last very long, and often end before it is very late in the night. The longest parties are usually in years of drought, after the harvests have come in and it is clear that there will be starvation. In these dismal seasons, our leaders are so disconsolate that they are almost unable to bear the burden of leadership. At such times, there are frequently more girls brought in for entertainment than there are leaders to entertain. Extreme worry at these times has been the cause of early death for many of our most illustrious leaders.

Although sometimes I am embarrassed to witness the proceedings at these parties—the oldest of our leaders seemingly always take the youngest of the girls—it is all harmless and, in fact, necessary to leadership. The occasions when I have the sad duty of escorting one of the girls to the soldiers outside to be returned to her home because she has displeased one of our leaders—as often as not, I have to lead her to the cold air before she is fully dressed and, invariably, she is in tears, perhaps from distress at having displeased her master of the moment, perhaps from distress at her prospective journey with the soldiers to her far-away village—these occasions are rare.

Already in my grandfather's time, the unfortunate practice of beating girls who displeased our leaders was ended. My father thought perhaps it was found that the beatings disrupted the revelry. Or perhaps the example of their peers' beatings served more to mortify the other girls than to render them more responsive. As is most likely, my father did not know the reasons for this wise action.

One of our oldest, most illustrious leaders is fond of smearing himself with honey and then asking one of the girls to lick him clean. One evening recently, a girl refused. He blinked in disbelief and then ordered her. She began to cry and did nothing. He tried to use force, also to no avail. Then he told me to drag her to the center of the hall and to beat her. I tried to console him, "Perhaps you would rather take another girl, your excellency." But he was adamant. I had dragged her from the beds and ordered a servant to bring me a whip when the matter drew the attention of several other leaders. The regulations forbidding the beating of the maids was not to be violated by me. His excellency's good sense got the better of him and, while the matter was discussed, I quickly led the whimpering maid to the soldiers at the door. In my haste, however, I forgot about her clothes, and only after she was gone did I realize that she had gone naked to her long journey home in the bitter cold. Fortunately, the soldiers had seemed eager for the journey—they had been standing around idly for several hours. Naked and in the cold she could at least be glad she had been spared a beating. But I was severely reprimanded for attempting to violate the regulations. Had they not one by one been distracted by other diversions of the evening, our leaders would probably have beaten me—there is no regulation against that. Why should the girl have denied his poor excellency his trivial pleasure? The two girls chosen to substitute for her showed much better sense, and demonstrated anew the wisdom of our leaders in their original decision. Beating an offending maid is unnecessary.

When I began to educate my son, however, my wife began to claim—maybe it is not so, our leaders are not wise, maybe; maybe self-serving; pleasure-seeking; tyrants, our leaders— that is the substance as well as the grammar of her complaint. I have tried to be patient, answering, "Do you wish to interfere with my son's learning grammar?" To my son I said only, "What do women know of leadership?"

This year has been a particularly difficult one for our leaders. Winter frost is in the air, in my untended fields, and still our leaders take refuge in our village. I am not quite sure how it came about, but a few days after I returned from a party which had lasted nearly a week, I described the party to my wife—not everything, fortunately, for how can the woman be made to understand aspects of leadership? Nevertheless, I was irresponsible. I had drunk wine after dinner, perhaps a bit too much, and I was tired. She teased the information out of me as we lay in bed and my mind was distracted. Perhaps her interest had been renewed when she met someone with a friend from a neighboring village, the mother of one of the girls enlisted for the entertainment of our leaders. She now insists that our leaders are selfish, immoral, crude—that they do not have the interests of the people at heart. I have wearied of quarreling with her on the subject of our leaders. I find her continued insistence disturbing, irritating. She makes it difficult for me to educate our son.

PEASANT GENIUS

Forgive my clumsy style, I have never before written, I am an ill-educated peasant, it was only recently discovered that I am almost inconceivably gifted, a genius they say. Before the discovery I hoed potatoes, now I am expected to become the leading physicist of the century. Or perhaps composer, or mathematician, or chess master, I have not yet finally decided, there is time, I began to study little more than two months ago, I still have much to learn.

It is fortunate that the discovery was made before it was too late, before I grew too old to begin a second life, I have my country to thank for the discovery. Like all young men, I had to report to the Army for service to the country, I was given an intelligence test, I could neither read nor write, I failed the test. The Army needed men at the time, I was called back for retesting, I said I had never learned to read. "Stupid peasant," the officer said. They tested me orally, I made a perfect score, no one had ever come close to a perfect score before. They tried other tests, all perfect or nearly perfect scores, after each test they muttered "Stupid peasant." Finally they decided I was gifted. They have now decided that I may serve the country through study rather than in the Army, no peasant had ever been exempted from the Army in order to study, they say I am exceptional, I am now being taught.

Two months ago they taught me to read and to write, last month they taught me grammar and began science and mathematics, this month they have also been teaching me philosophy. Fortunately, I learn fast, else all the learning would take so long that my gifted mind could never finally be put to original creative use. At first my lessons were given at the school in the village near my home, soon I surpassed the knowledge and intelligence of the teacher there, now my instruction is given in private tutorials at the university in the city, of course I cannot immediately be admitted to the classes with the other students, they are not peasants, they have never been peasants.

To be gifted entails many things which one would never have related to intellect, if one is gifted one must dress well, speak well, have perfect manners, it is not an easy thing to be a genius. I have read of other geniuses who do not dress well, who do not have proper manners, they are all older geniuses, perhaps when I am older, I too. To master the standards of dress, manners, and speech, this is a minor problem, even a peasant could learn such standards. What is difficult is not to learn the standards but to apply them, the difficulty is that I can no longer wear the same clothes day and night, I can no longer piss out the window, I can no longer say piss (they have said nothing against writing it, of course I had never written it before, perhaps therefore it is permitted now, or perhaps there simply are no standards for writing). Fortunately with my intellect I am able to reconcile myself to the burdens involved in the application of my newly learned standards, I have even grown accustomed to bathing. I no longer ache for potatoes and bread, I am satisfied with meat. The very gifts which genius implies make the burdens of genius bearable, moreover it is an honor to serve the country in the exacting life of a student instead of in the pleasant life of a soldier in the fields.

The life of a genius is not all bad. Still, it is not without grievous personal difficulties that one can make the transition from peasanthood to genius, perhaps I belabor the obvious, if so please forgive me, perhaps I should merely give examples. One example is my fiancée, Maria. When she heard I would study, Maria was pleased, she hoped we would not have to be peasants. What an odd reaction, Maria despises all who are not peasants, yet she wishes not to be a peasant. I asked her, "Can one intelligently wish to be what he would not like?" She did not answer, I wonder, had she begun to despise me? I tried to teach her to be the fiancée of a genius, it was no use, she is still the fiancée of a peasant. Try this (it is a syllogism in the manner of Aristotle, who was a Greek philosopher, that is, a "lover of wisdom," Greeks frequently have a single name): I am not a peasant, Maria is the fiancée of a peasant ... conclusion? Maria is not my fiancée. For proof, I tried to explain the syllogism to Maria. Did she understand? Of course not, the peasant could only understand the conclusion, not the premises, how can one be so backward? (I am sorry, I have not explained all of the technical terminology, the *premises* are the first two statements in the syllogism.) But I fear that Maria has reason, the conclusion follows.

I have given one example, another example is my mother, Mama. After the Army told her that I should leave home to study, Mama used to say to me, "Son, you don't want that, live in a dirty old city? Why this farm is yours when Papa dies, who in that old city ever had himself a farm?" I agreed with her, do not be surprised, how could I have known what it meant to be a genius? But the Army came back and said I could be in the Army or study to be a genius. It is in the nature of genius that one can understand what it is to be one only if one is. One who is not simply cannot understand what it means, Mama has not understood, one can understand her even if she cannot understand us.

But I do not like to see Mama anymore, she only quarrels, who wishes to take a long trip home when there are only quarrels to be got? Besides, I have little time to spare from my studies, I have increasing difficulty understanding Papa's and Mama's peasant accent, my brothers and sisters all mock me. Their reaction is only natural, still it is unpleasant for me, those of us who are educated expect discussion to be rational, we deplore bickering, though I can understand my family (I can even empathize, I am not so far removed from peasantry myself), I cannot tolerate their ignorant quarreling, it seems they did not quarrel so much before.

When I was taking lessons at the school in the village near our home, I used to explain to Mama why I studied, at that time I did not have to explain it to Maria. Maria understood, perhaps because she was also young, or maybe she understood wrong, she did not understand at all, she only seemed to understand. Mama did not even seem to understand, perhaps that is a difference of age, the young seem, the old can no longer seem, or they have given up seeming. Now I think Mama was right, why did I think I was able to explain why I studied? I studied, that much was fact, "why" is no fact, it only seemed to me that I was explaining. Actually to explain, I would have had to know already then what I would know only after studying, that is a logical impossibility, it is such logical impossibilities which are the source of suicide. One would not explain one's study as preparation for suicide, it merely happens that one who has studied might choose suicide in preference to further life knowing what he has learned from his study.

Sad, it is only this logical impossibility which allows one to study his way to suicide. If one could know already what one can know only after studying, perhaps no one would study. With such knowledge peasants could be happy to be peasants, Maria would not suffer the envy she suffers, Mama would not quarrel with me, her son. But it is not so, one cannot know without study, Mama and Maria have not studied, they cannot know how dismal is the lot of those who are ignorant, the lot of peasants. I have studied, I can understand Maria's confused desires to be that which she despises, I can understand Mama's quarreling.

Perhaps that is wrong, perhaps I cannot understand Maria or Mama, yes I know I was also once a peasant, on the other hand I am no longer. My thought processes are a mystery to them, they cannot duplicate thoughts such as mine, their minds are not structured in the way of genius. Perhaps I can also not duplicate their thoughts, oh I can think I duplicate their thoughts, but I must suppress my own gifted insights in the process, perhaps it is impossible, my mind is not structured in the way of peasantry.

I am sorry, I am not quite sure just what I have said there, it is only natural that I, not so long ago a wholly ignorant peasant, should still be ignorant of the full implications of some of my thoughts. That is one of the problems my philosophy tutor has recently raised: can one express thoughts which he does not understand? Further still, can one join a conversation and respond in normal, even correct fashion, so that the other person in the conversation thinks one is understanding and yet it be the case that one is understanding nothing, not even the single words?

Silly question perhaps, yes, but then not. Maybe I have merely been trained to put the words together in the way of intelligible sentences and to make the right sentences to hold up my half of our conversation, after all, I am thought to be extremely gifted, that is partly what it means to be gifted, to make the right sentences. If that were all it meant, it would seem trivial to be gifted, that is a thought which I must explore further some time, not now, clearly there must be other aspects of being gifted, else the Army's intelligence tests could not differentiate and I would not be at the university but would be in the Army or at home hoeing. Perhaps again I belabor the obvious, I am sorry, I know what is obvious to me, it will take longer for me to learn from experience what is obvious to others, especially those who are neither geniuses nor peasants.

I used to wonder why I was selected for study, at first I was sure it was because I was expected to be a genius, now I realize that was not at all the reason, no, the reason I was selected was that I was a peasant. No peasant ever studies. Why? one wonders, yes, why? Clearly if I, not so long ago a peasant, can have asked such a question, the State must have asked the question long before. After generations of asking itself "Why?" the State must finally have decided to intervene, with the help of the Army the State found a peasant who could be induced to study.

The State must now be deeply pleased, it can be expected that henceforth even more peasants will study, when all have opportunity to study it will no longer be necessary to differentiate between peasants and not-peasants (according to one of the logical axioms of Aristotle, these two categories include everyone, that is to say they "exhaust the universe"), there will be no need to differentiate between those who do not study and those who do study (it is perhaps more difficult to see the logic, but these two categories also exhaust the universe). Until now these two categorizations have been virtually identical, the peasants were incompetent on their own to overcome the identity between themselves and those who do not study, and it is understandable that those who do study would not care to eliminate the identity between themselves as those who do study and as those who are not-peasants. These identities seemed unlikely to disappear of their own accord, the State must finally have decided to eliminate the identities by direct intervention. Now no peasant need despair, in our country even a peasant can rise above his origins, for instance consider me.

Perhaps one would feel that these distinctions are not meaningful, peasants and not-peasants, we are all citizens, I understand such a feeling, that is what I thought when the Army selected me. Soon I learned better, there was no denying I was still more peasant than not-peasant, I myself revealed it—my teacher at the village school admonished me, "We don't pick our noses," I misunderstood, I thought he was making comparisons, I answered, "Oh, *we* do, how funny." "Yes, isn't it?" he said. Later I realized. Now that I am here at the university it is clear that I am more not-peasant, though still somewhat peasant, it is not so quickly gone, it is especially hard to quit picking one's nose, I do not fret, there is time.

So long as I am still somewhat peasant, the other students can tell the difference. But they are kind, they point out my peasant mistakes with friendly laughing. To remind me that I must learn diligently they call me "Peasant," they avoid using my name. With their help I will overcome my origins, I too will be in the category of not-peasants, it will be an honor finally to be allowed to attend the classes with the other students.

By that attitude I do not mean to criticize peasants, I think there are aspects of the peasant life which are good. After dinner with my fellow students last night I was wishing for a while that I could still be a peasant. It was late, we had drunk, I had eaten several helpings of beans, I said, "If only we could be peasants for the rest of the night, it would be beautiful." They all stared at me, no one said a word, the two who were drinking put down their wine glasses, the one who was eating dropped his fork. Finally one of them asked, "O.K., Peasant, what would be beautiful about being a peasant?"

Then I realized, they could not know. "Well," I said, "at least we would have a cow nearby."

They all laughed, one of them kept cackling "Oh Peasant," they are friendly that way. They insisted cows are not necessary in the city, they have promised this weekend to take me to some "civilized cow substitutes." Perhaps they are right, perhaps there is nothing beautiful about being a peasant, I cannot yet say, I will not go home this weekend, I want to see how it is with the city's cow substitutes.

It seems that being a student is not as bad as peasants think, but perhaps I am merely fortunate, my fellow students might be unusually generous. I had not got to know them very well until the dinner last night. They surprised me by bringing food for all of us to my room, they drank a toast to me before the meal, "To the peasant, Let's all eat like peasants." The meal was only beans, beautiful beans, not since I left home had I enjoyed a meal so much, to eat like a peasant again, I was deeply moved by the thoughtfulness of my fellow students.

When we finished eating all the beans, they drank another toast, "To the peasant, Now let's all fart like peasants." Afterwards I could hardly sleep, the stink nearly drove me from my bed, I was no longer accustomed to it, it was too cold to open my window. At home I slept with my sisters and brothers, I was the oldest, my sisters took turns lying beside me, they kept me warm even with the windows open. Here I sleep alone, with the window open I would freeze, again I revealed that I am still somewhat peasant, I chose to stink rather than freeze.

This morning my tutor refused to continue the lesson, "You reek like a goatherd," he said and sent me away to walk in the fresh air and take a bath. I have understood, I am grateful for the lesson, my fellow students were willing to subject themselves to the stink of peasants all for my benefit, I try now to stop farting. It is hard for me to comprehend how peasants live with themselves, especially in cold weather when the windows are closed.

I walked in the fresh air, I bathed, I put on clean clothes, and I returned to my tutor. I apologized for my earlier odor and began the day's lesson all in a single observation, an observation I had deduced from the day's philosophy assignment. I said, "One is what one is." Forgive me, it sounds obvious, especially to peasants, but it is not obvious, not to philosophers, it is a profound insight (it is the task of philosophers to have profound insights, that distinguishes them from mere peasants). My philosophy tutor is not a very good philosopher (therefore he is a tutor), he does not like the idea that one is what one is, he does not like the idea that he is what he is, he wishes he were an ancient Greek, or better still a Medieval priest, he says he is not happy to be in his time.

I told him, that is crazy, how can one wish to be what he is not, then he would not be he. I said, "You can think such a thing only because you are in your time." He answered, "Yes, you are right of course. That is the difference between one who is happy in his time and one who is not."

A true tutor, he congratulates me for my reasoning while denying my conclusion. What more can one say to him? What good does it do him that he has learned not to fart? His own years of study were in vain, he is a tutor, he will always be a tutor.

MY OWN COMMAND

I was given my own command. I admit that in the thick of war it is possible to rise higher than one really deserves, but precisely therefore I have been all the more inclined to demonstrate that I deserved the trust shown in me—not that the command was either very difficult or very important, but the lives of many men were given over to my will, and that alone would justify the dedication I have put into fulfilling my orders. But even more important than the lives of my men and myself—what are we, a mere handful, compared to the life of the fatherland—was the realization that each outpost was in a sense all outposts, for if one outpost fell, the path was open and the heart of the fatherland was bared to the enemy. Clearly, one should not underrate the importance of the task even if one were inclined to dismiss the significance of my elevation to the command. Nor its difficulty, for my orders were as brief as a logical proposition and almost as inclusive: "Defend the outpost of the fatherland against any assault by the enemy until receipt of countermanding orders." I have received no countermanding orders, and although our supplies are running low and some of the men occasionally seemto lose faith in the fatherland, as long as I am in command, we will obey the orders we have been given.

Perhaps that was a slight overstatement—the men do not so much lose faith in the fatherland, they only wonder sometimes whether it has forgotten them (indeed, although I would never let the men think so, sometimes I have almost wondered myself). And I certainly would not wish to give the impression that I have any difficulty maintaining control or that there is ever the slightest notion of rebellion, because even if the fatherland had forgotten us, it could nonetheless still be confident in its last thought of us that none of my men would forget it: the fatherland need not lose faith in us, we fulfill our orders. For as long as we have been here, none of the enemy has ever dared within the range of our weapons—the enemy has even built a fence slightly beyond our range, perhaps to protect his children from straying into our line of fire, perhaps to pretend that we are not here, as though he had no enemy. But, perhaps because the fence is there, so far we have been able to fulfill our mission without firing a shot.

My men often discuss the fence—it is by far the most common theme in their conversation. They quarrel whether it is there to protect the enemy's children or to hide the truth of our commanding presence, and I think most of them agree that it is to protect the children. However, I would maintain that it is definitely there to hide the truth (although I would never enter into the discussions of my men—not only is there a certain distance which I, as the commanding officer, must keep, there is also no harm in leaving the question unsettled among them in order to leave them something of such clear interest to occupy their time), for ours is a proud enemy, and in his pride he cannot admit his failings to himself.

Yes, I know that I make that claim on what seems to be very little evidence since we have had no contact with the enemy, but in truth there is overwhelming evidence. It is not merely that he would build a fence to hide from himself the truth, there are also other customs of the enemy which betray his pride. For instance, he does not live in the sort of dwellings, comfortable but humble, with which our people are satisfied; rather, the enemy builds fine houses, each new one larger and more opulent than the last. One could almost say that his pride is boundless (except that there is, of course, the fence), because his houses now block the view around our outpost in all directions; we can see only the fence, the houses which rise above it, and the sky. Perhaps it is that view which most often leads some of my men to wonder whether the fatherland has forgotten us.

A WAR OF RESPECT

Ours is a war of respect. We do not indulge in petty hatred, in a trivial contest for territory, or in blind antagonism. No. We fight out of the respect each of us, my people and our enemy, has developed for the courage and tenacity of the other.

Over the years we have grown to esteem each other as perhaps few adversaries in all the history of civilized warfare, and I think I can say without exaggeration—it is the simple truth—that respect is well deserved on both sides. Neither of us has ever quit the field while still able to attack, so that all of our encounters have ended in the exhaustion and incapacitation of both our armies. It has not been seldom that my people have feared for their existence under our enemy's blows, and I doubt that our enemy would consider me presumptuous to say that he has just as often had occasion to wonder whether he could survive.

Our first encounter was generations ago (the histories do not specify exactly when). Some details of it are clearly recorded in the histories, others are blurred by contradictory legends. The surest fact is that it was one of our most brutal battles, although later battles can hardly be described as less brutal. The struggle lasted so long that when my people prevailed, we were too exhausted to use our advantage—or perhaps my people did not really prevail so much as that we both suffered exhaustion simultaneously. In any case, it was

clear to our forefathers—and I suspect to our enemy as well—
that there would be another meeting, and that expectation of
"the next time" has only grown stronger over the years after
each encounter.

Recently we learned that the people of our enemy were
torn with strife. Several youths had captured the enemy's
council of elders and had attempted to usurp their rule. For
several days it appeared that the enemy would be incapable
of organizing his forces to protect himself against attack.
When we received this news, we were thrown into debating
whether we should quickly attack when victory would be assured. One of our younger elders advocated attack: "At last
we can gain victory and insure peace. Then our sons need no
longer die in battle. Then our women would not sleep alone
in their later years. I say, Attack now, Win now, Peace now!"

But others disagreed. One elder, who is wont to admonish
us lest we fail to see the real reasons behind any action,
rhetorically questioned the younger elder, "And how do we
know we will gain the victory? Has any of us been in the
enemy's homeland to see him torn with factions? Or do we
merely accept the word of a wandering vagabond, a hireling,
perhaps, of the council of elders of our enemy? No, my fellow
elders, peace will be ours only if we have the cunning of
patience."

Our debate became woefully acrimonious, and we were unable to agree on any action before we heard that the rebellious
youths of our enemy had been put down and their leaders ex-
ecuted. Even as we listened to this news, we were surprised
by an attack from our enemy, and we only narrowly survived
a hard fought battle in the heart of our capital.

Afterwards, some of our people complained that because
we had not attacked in the propitious moment, we had nearly
met destruction. But in the style of the rhetorical elder one

might ask, Would not such a cowardly act have violated our enemy's respect? We are not at war merely on the quest for victory, but on the quest for honorable victory. Honor is a function not of ends but of means. Our respect for our enemy and his for us are founded not on expectations of victory and defeat, but on realizations of courage and tenacity in battle. Our council of elders honorably did not decide to take advantage of our enemy's difficulties of the moment.

However, our enemy should not expect that it will always be so. We cannot sacrifice our advantage every time he is weakened by internal strife. To do so is to risk strife among our own people, not least because our respect for the enemy is greatest when he seems weakest. A paradox, the idea seems ridiculous, one might accuse me of sophistry. But no, further thought suggests that, no matter how often we have gained the upper hand, no matter how often he has been incapacitated, he has always come back to gain the advantage over us. Hence our fear is greatest in moments of victory, without hidden meaning I can genuinely claim that our respect grows as our adversary weakens. And I would not be surprised if he were to say the same of us.

During the past year our mutual respect has grown beyond the bounds of expression, it has reached proportions that I would have considered superhuman only a year ago, and I think no one but my people and our enemy could comprehend it—in fact, I admit it is probably beyond my understanding. Our rate of attrition has become catastrophic—we cannot sustain it much longer. If the enemy's losses had not been equally as great, we would have no hope of eventual victory or even survival. Though our conflict has continued over many generations, in the twenty-three years I have lived, it has become increasingly severe. Not so much severe, I should say, as merely frequent. In my grandfather's time, the encounters were still so rare that he did not actually see one until he was old enough to participate. He had believed that the tales of our enemy were a great legend, part of the folklore of our people. But so great is the advantage which accrues to the initiator of any particular battle that the time between our encounters has grown increasingly shorter. By the time my father fell in battle, the encounters had become almost annual. Little more than a year ago they began to be monthly; with the attack which we have planned for today, they will have become almost daily.

When we both retired incapacitated and exhausted from the field yesterday, there was perhaps no one among us who doubted that we would both be on the attack this morning, even though neither of us has many men still alive who are not too crippled for combat. For the past several weeks many of the women among my people have been murmuring that the end must soon come, else we will all perish. Last night they claimed that a further encounter today would surely end the long and respected history of our people. Perhaps. But the council of elders decided nonetheless that our best hope for survival lay in initiating the attack today.

In that action we can probably not hope to surprise our adversary, but at least we cannot be surprised by him. To surprise him, we have armed our women and children and joined them with us in today's attack. If our enemy has not done the same, our survivors will tonight celebrate the final victory in our war of respect. Our enemy will have no men left to bury his filthy dead, who will rot upon the field while we proceed to the slaughter of his women and children. My people will live in peace.

KEEPER OF THE RULES

I am the Keeper of the Rules of State. I think it is not an exaggeration to say that the single most important reason our state is governed more equitably and less capriciously than any other state in recorded history is that our Legislators early saw the need for instituting a Keeper of the Rules. The Keeper edits the roughly drafted edicts of the Legislators to put them into corrected final form in order that they may enter the Rules of State with syntax and linguistic usage in common with all past Rules of State. Hence our Judges can refer to a single, coherent body of rules when they sit in judgment over citizens.

But it is recently being argued by some of the Legislators that the State has outgrown the need of a Keeper of the Rules. One of the leaders of this dissension has said repeatedly, "We vote edicts which the Keeper then edits for syntax, and when he returns the edited versions to us to enter into the Rules of State"—at this point he frequently almost yells—"we do not recognize the Keeper's final drafts, we cannot find in them the substance of the edicts which we have voted."

He is a moderate. There are others, especially among the younger Legislators, who, because they are not yet versed in the affairs of state, seldom have opportunity or courage to speak on issues of substance, and hence occupy themselves with attacking me. When their philosophical arguments do not impress their elders, they can occasionally be heard mumbling slanderous references to the quality of my editing. They declare openly that I deliberately change the meanings of their edicts.

It is not true that I change the meanings of their edicts—it is merely that they do not fully understand the meanings, that they do not fully understand logic and syntax. (The Legislators are less well-educated today than they were in past generations. It is only therefore that the rough drafts of their edicts require what they call "heavy editing.") Although, as I have hinted, the Keeper of the Rules is perhaps the most important institution of the Government, the Legislators still, as always, promulgate the edicts. It is not true that, as one of them—M, I think—likes to exaggerate, "The Keeper has become the Government."

Why Keep the Rules?

Why did our early Legislators so wisely establish a Keeper? They were concerned with the self-apparent problems inherent in writing the rules of writing, as it were, in the very language whose use those rules were to govern. They foresaw circularities, endless disputes of linguistic interpretation which would only vitiate the very Rules of State which the rules of writing were supposed to clarify. It was realized that the rules governing the writing of state edicts could only be embodied in a Keeper, who must be reared into the rules through an apprenticeship to the present Keeper, an apprenticeship of decades during which the apprentice would participate in all editing done by the Keeper and would receive instruction as well.

The task of keeping the Rules was soon found to demand the Keeper's full attention. Hence it was early promulgated that "The Keeper of the Rules shall remain celibate and shall remain at all hours of all days in Quarters to be provided for him in the Hall of Legislators in order that he be not distracted from the performance of his duties." (Were I editing that edict today, I think its wording would be slightly different, although its meaning would not be essentially changed, merely the Keeper would be left some freedom.)

Later generations added to the original edict establishing the Keeper of the Rules. To summarize many pages of addenda, it is stipulated that the Keeper shall have no contact with any person except his apprentice (it was feared that the Keeper could be bribed). Hence the Keeper's Quarters—which are both sumptuous and spartan (my predecessor found them sumptuous, I find them spartan)—are completely closed off from the remainder of the Hall and have neither windows nor doors, with the exception of the short, narrow door through which every generation a new apprentice enters and a deceased Keeper's body exits. All food and other supplies enter through elaborate chutes which are opened only when several servants and Governors simultaneously operate locked controls in many different locations in the Hall. The rough drafts of newly adopted edicts enter through a chute directly linking the Chamber of Legislators to the Quarters of the Keeper. The edited final drafts are returned to the Legislators through the same chute, and simultaneously—to prevent duplicity on the part of the Legislators—they are passed through another chute directly to the Chamber of Judges in the neighboring Hall of Justice.

Here is the chute to the Chamber of Legislators, there on the other wall is the chute to the Chamber of Judges. The Judges and the Legislators are linked, as it were, by this room, the Keeper's Office—this is my chamber, I daresay, my

Chamber. At this desk I edit, by my hand edicts become Rules of State in order that justice may be done by a uniform standard.

My predecessor argued that the principal function of the Keeper is to write the Rules in the fine Script of State so that they will be uniformly legible. He pointed out that most of an apprentice's time is spent in practicing this Script, not in learning rules of syntax. But, I submit, if the Keeper were a mere scribe, he would not require the elaborate devices which protect him, there would be no need for him to wear the robes which I wear, a single smock would be adequate to his task. My predecessor was not wrong, of course. Our slightly different views merely reflect an alternation in emphasis which is typical of successive Keepers. My predecessor's predecessor agreed with me, his predecessor's predecessor agreed with him.

The Ladder to Syntactical Purity

Technically speaking, I am the Keeper of the Rules of State because I embody the rules of syntax, logic, and linguistic usage according to which the Rules of State are drafted in their published and legally binding form. Perhaps it is not surprising that this strict sense of the title has become confused over the generations so that today I am more often construed to be the keeper of the rules of syntax than Keeper of the Rules of State. It is ironic, however, that just this confusion underlies the necessity of my position. One cannot "keep" the rules of syntax and linguistic usage—if that were possible, there would be no need of a "keeper." The very reason it is necessary to have a Keeper of the Rules of State is that the rules of syntax cannot be kept, but can only be embodied in their actual application.

Perhaps another reason for the confusion surrounding my title is that, originally, the Keeper kept the Rules in the most literal sense of the word—the final versions of the Rules as edited by him were bound and placed on shelves in his Quarters, where Judges, Legislators, and legal scholars could refer to them. That was, of course, before it was decided to protect the institution of the Keeper—as well as the integrity of the Rules—by preventing contact between Judges, Legislators, and the Keeper. Even after the edict isolating the Keeper from the influence of other officials of the Hall, the Rules were still kept in the Keeper's Quarters.

Eventually, however, it was argued that some keepers (I will not name names—there was never any proof given for any of the allegations, which were therefore, according to the Rules of State, slanderous), it was argued that some keepers applied not merely the rules of syntax, logic, and linguistic usage to the edicts of the Legislators; rather, far more they applied the past Rules of State, thereby effectively preventing any alternations or accretions to the Rules of State. (According to the rules of syntax and linguistic usage, these two terms are, of course, identical—alterations are accretions—but I am representing the stated claims of dissident Legislators rather than the actual substance of their claims, so I have not edited.)

It was decided that in order to insure that the Keeper edit only for syntax, logic, and linguistic usage, the past Rules of State should be removed from his Quarters. Many subsequent Keepers have suspected (rightly, I am sure) that this edict could not have survived in its final form if the rules of syntax had been rigorously applied to it. Perhaps a bribe, an occasional woman guest, induced the Keeper at that time to allow the edict to pass with inadequate editing. Shame I feel, as of hot and cold water pouring over me at the thought that even one rule could have been permitted into the Rules of State with improper syntax, that a keeper of the Rules of State could have been guilty of collusion with Legislators, that corrupt editing could have been done at the desk at which I now sit.

And yet, it seems to me that this rule, established however shamefully, is the essential underpinning of the institution of the Keeper of the Rules. Without it, no Keeper could be fully confident that he embodied the rules of syntax rather than merely parroting from past Rules of State. And just that distinction is the whole point of a Keeper of the Rules. It is ironic that the institution of a Keeper could be achieved in its most perfect form only by the violation of the Keeper's duties, even if only in a single instance (there is not the slightest hint that there has ever been another violation—if one dismisses the more grotesque assertions of some of today's younger Legislators against me). That one violation is, as it were, the ladder by which the Keeper is able to climb from a base and common existence as a mere mimic—an educated and highly sophisticated mimic to be sure, but still a mimic—to the splendid essence of philosophical, syntactical—dare I say purity? Hence, even as I feel shame that the rule was allowed past the Keeper's editing, I rejoice that it is enforced.

A Threatening Edict

One senses from all this history an almost organic growth as is not untypical of the legal codes of states. However, it does not take prolonged thought among those educated in such matters to perceive that in the institutions of our state, the process of growth has reached a culmination, a logical wholeness, a perfection of the sort toward which all good states might seem to be groping, now progressing, now stumbling back, but never really nearing the end of the development. Most states succumb—either to the attack of enemies from without or to the nibbling of enemies from within—long before they achieve even the beginnings of good institutions.

But we, or our forefathers, have established essentially perfect institutions, and the day when that perfection was finally attained was, I submit, the day when the edict removing the Rules of State from my Quarters—or rather from the Quarters of the Keeper of the Rules of State—was passed. It was the last of the edicts governing actual forms of the institutions of the State ever voted. Only recently has any Legislator seriously proposed new alterations in those institutions.

I was horrified when I realized what the Legislators intended—as indeed even any good simple citizen would have been had he known and had he been able to understand the issues involved. The Legislators voted an edict which I thought could alter our institutions—but fortunately, after I read it carefully enough to edit it for final entry into the Rules of State, I found that it did not in fact alter the institutions. Needless to say, I was pleased, but my pleasure was greatest not merely at the fact that the institutions remained unaltered, but rather at the fact that the institutions demonstrated themselves to be their own greatest safeguard against alteration. I now almost dare to believe that our state is perfected against the possibility of nibbling destruction from within.

The edict which the Legislators voted said that editing by the Keeper should not be so severe that three fourths of the Legislators should not remember what was the original point of their passing the edict when they read it in edited form. Clearly, the wording of that edict was so confusing as to require very careful reworking lest it be open to grievous misinterpretation and misapplication. I worked the whole night just to outline the actual content of the rough draft of the edict and then spent the following day writing the edited final draft to go into the Rules of State.

This edict involved a profound philosophical problem of the sort which had originally led to the institution of the Keeper. That problem can best be stated as a question: How can a rule be construed to apply to itself? If that problem could not be resolved, the edict could not be elevated to a Rule of State. Happily, I was able to resolve the problem although, unhappily, many Legislators, old as well as young, were not entirely pleased with the edict which they discovered they had promulgated.

At the session in which I returned the edited version of this edict to the Legislators, the Chairman of Legislators had to gavel the day's meeting to a close already in the early morning. After he had fixed the edict into the current volume of the Rules, further business became impossible when a virtual chorus of the younger Legislators began to moan, "But we are not able to call into question the Keeper's decisions—why should that be?"

Old questions, old problems.

How odd it is that the solution to one problem becomes then (in the view of the simple-minded) the new problem whose solution is found in the resurrection of the original problem. That foolish regression is commonly the result of a change of generations. But in the present case we should not let ourselves be deceived. No, the solution to the original problem is not itself a problem. It may be hard for Legislators to live with it, but it is not a problem, because I make no decisions, I only embody the rules of syntax. If the plaint of the Legislators were put into proper syntax, it would be "But we are not able to call into question the Keeper's *editing*. . ." Now this plaint is at least correct, even if it is sad from the point of view of some legislators. Indeed, as our forefathers foresaw, no one else knows the rules of syntax—only I, the Keeper, am qualified to judge whether I have adhered to them.

However, the philosophizing Legislators claim that this is not so—they claim that it would not be possible in fact for anyone else actually to learn the rules of syntax which apply and to be able to apply them with results equivalent to my results, that is to say, with uniquely uniform syntax. This contention is clearly equivalent to saying that I do not edit according to rules at all—that I edit by caprice, by whim, that I would get one result if I edit today's edict today, another result altogether if I wait until tomorrow. I might as well be a poet, a spinner of tales—dare I say, I might as well be a Legislator.

But my detractors counter their own arguments, for on other occasions they insist that I edit according to a coherent political creed so that all edicts in their edited forms consistently support that creed. That is to say I edit by political rules. Now either I edit according to rules or I do not—one does not require education in philosophy to understand that tautology.

There are moments when I would like nothing better than to yell through the chute linking my Quarters to the Chamber of Legislators, "Which is it, Legislators—do I edit according to rules, or do I not?"

"The Living Language"

Perhaps it is this misunderstanding which is the source of one of the strangest arguments of my detractors. They claim that there is no coherent, clear, and unambiguous language in which to keep the Rules of State. Why? Because the language has sense only in the context of the life of the people, and the people are not a coherent, clear, and unambiguous army of syntactical automata. An incredible proposition—and their peers among the Legislators do not say merely, "Shut up, young fools, sit down—we have heard enough of your patter today."

Let us carry their argument to its logical conclusion (but note that if their argument were coherent, then according to its own premise, it would have no logical conclusion, we could deduce nothing from it, indeed we could not even deduce that we could deduce nothing from it—such deductions we can make only because their argument is not correct, and because we do have a coherent language in which to discuss their arguments and to make correct deductions from them). Their notion of "the living language" implies that the function of the Legislators is merely to string together words, which the Judges then cause to mean whatever they wish them to mean in each case which comes before them—that is to say, *the Judges are the Government.* Yet these philosophers use their argument to support the claim—which would be meaningless in their system—that I, the Keeper, am the Government.

As is often the case, however, the complaint of the young Legislators is not wholly without a hint of foundation—even the babbling of fools frequently betrays its kernel of truth, however obscured that kernel might be. It happens, of course, that the truth at the core of the Legislators' complaint is a very minor truth, but as befits one whose life's work is the non-partisan correction of poor syntax, let me peel away the verbiage from their complaint and reveal its kernel of truth, let me even provide an example which instantiates that truth.

First the example. It happens that I know the arguments of the Legislators even though their arguments per se are never written into their edicts.

How?

Well, I overhear them. The chute which connects my Quarters with their Chamber suffers from faulty construction, so that the door at my end of the chute has been broken since shortly after my predecessor died. Technically, the door is supposed to open only twice each day for one minute at each opening—once for me to remove edicts which the Legislators have placed there and once for me to place there the final drafts of the Rules of State. To my surprise, I discovered once while removing a day's edicts that the door at the other end of the chute is by itself not soundproof. And very soon thereafter, my door ceased to close. Happily, to my knowledge there is no Rule against my listening to the Legislators— probably because it was assumed to be impossible, but assumptions are not Rules.

And now to the kernel of truth in the complaint of the philosophizing Legislators. Despite the fact that my listening to the Legislators' debates perhaps violates the spirit (though not the letter) of the Rules, it enables me to maintain that contact with the language in its organic existence without which I could not hope to remain a coherent link between the language as used in the rough draft edicts of the Legislators and the language as established in the rules of syntax. To carry this point further to insist that only through contact with what these philosophers call "the living language" can one understand the meaning of their edicts—that is a mindless abstraction.

Perhaps now that the subject has arisen, I should better explain the chance fact that I overhear the debates of the Legislators. Overhearing the debates often makes it possible for me to serve my function better, for there are occasions when I would not know so clearly how wrong is the syntax of their edicts if I did not hear their claims in the debates during which the edicts are drafted. Frequently, it is the case that an edict does not include statements specifying the realm in which it is expected to apply. It gives no explanation of why the Legislators selected just this edict and this wording. Only in the debates are such topics addressed. And yet, without knowing these things, one cannot genuinely claim to know what an edict means—indeed it is perhaps not an exaggeration to say that one should not ask what an edict means, but should ask only how it is to be applied. This very point is often enough made by my detractors when they wish to show how misdirected is the institution of a Keeper. But these philosophers write edicts which are supposed to have meaning in the absence of any explanation or description of the sorts of circumstances in which they might be expected to apply.

The Paper Restrictions

Given that their logic is frequently so spurious, perhaps it is not surprising that many Legislators, especially the younger ones on the rare occasions when they finally submit bills of their own, wish to legislate things which cannot be legislated—syntax forbids them. Nonetheless, sometimes their bills become edicts, and then comes my most painful task. I cannot simply say, "No, this cannot be legislated," and then submit a detailed explanation. I can only edit. Unfortunately, I must then return to them the final drafts of these edicts to enter the Rules of State, and they sense that I have altered their intent.

There was a time when that was not a problem—the older Legislators were as convinced as I am that their younger peers were somewhat foolish from lack of experience, and that they simply misremembered what they had proposed. The younger Legislators could never convince the older ones because the Rules do not permit Legislators to keep copies of their rough draft edicts. The Legislators are supposed to have their supply of paper severely restricted. Each Legislator is allowed as many sheets of paper as he wishes when he enters the Chamber of Legislators at the beginning of a day's session, but the number of sheets is carefully recorded, and at the end of the session he must surrender all of it, whether used or not, to be destroyed. This restriction serves a useful purpose, which is to prevent the taking of permanent notes which might then be used to offer alternative interpretations of the Rules of State.

However, I know that some of the Legislators have begun— in violation of the Rules—to make their own personal copies of the rough draft edicts in order to be able to compare them with the edited drafts which I return to them. I can hear excited, angry murmuring immediately as soon as the edited versions are taken from the chute which connects their Chamber to my Quarters. So far I have attempted to maintain my necessarily strict standards of editing despite all the complaints which—unknown to them—I overhear. However, one cannot be certain of one's ability to suppress subconscious efforts to avoid unnecessary criticism—on minor edicts, especially on those not relating specifically to the rules of syntax or to the institution of the Keeper of the Rules, I am sometimes fearful that I might edit too leniently. But I redouble my efforts in such cases—I uphold the standards according to the rules. If I did not, no one else would know.

I suspect that some of the Legislators plan to trick me by submitting the same edict twice to show that the edited versions differ, thereby proving that I do *not* edit according to genuine rules. The only problem for them—even assuming the absurd result that I did actually edit the "two" edicts differently—would be to show their peers that the rough draft edicts were identical. To do so, they would obviously have to admit, nay, proclaim that they were keeping records of the rough drafts. It is then that they would encounter my natural allies, the older Legislators, who would not want to know that their speeches and arguments could also be recorded by their adversaries to be used against them in power struggles among the Legislators.

The older Legislators stand to lose as much as I, although their loss would not unequivocally be also a loss to the State. They, too, wish not to have their potential opponents make detailed records of their speeches from which a coherent picture of their views could be constructed to make a coherent attack against them possible. I know that, so far, it is only this consideration which has prevented the younger Legislators from actually attempting to trick me. Sad—these younger Legislators have not the courage to attack all their enemies at once, yet such is the logic of their weapons that they cannot attack us singly.

In the meantime, the younger Legislators have reduced themselves to the status of stenographers, fitfully trying to record every word spoken, every edict promulgated in rough draft by the Legislators. Sadly, I fear that I must follow their example, although here the deceitful Legislators clearly have great advantages over me. They can easily enough smuggle contraband paper into the sessions, whereas the regulations against my having extra paper are, because of the nature of things, highly effective. If the younger Legislators were to

46

overcome their timidity long enough to attempt to trick me into editing the same edict twice, my lack of extra paper could be a severe handicap. Not that I grant that my editing is not done according to genuine rules of syntax, but it is always possible that I might be ill or tired from overwork and perhaps could err, however, slightly, a chance my detractors could then seize upon as proof of my inconsistency.

There appears to be no hope that I might be able to obtain extra paper. I must discharge as many sheets of paper each week as I have been given, and it appears that no Keeper has yet found a way to get around this stipulation. Therefore, the only standard available to me in my task of editing is the standard which I have acquired from my predecessor. However, there is one slight loophole in the system: in order to enable the Keeper to work over the weekend if he so chooses, one extra sheet of paper has been allotted to him for all time. I have therefore lately been working on a system of shorthand writing which I have now nearly perfected. I think I will soon forego the luxury of having an extra sheet for carrying work over Sundays in order to keep records of some of the edicts. To some degree I suppose one might plausibly assert that this practice might be counter to the intention of the rules disallowing the Keeper possession of a copy of the Rules of State, but on the other hand there is no explicit rule (at least not to my knowledge, and that is the disadvantage inherent in my not having a set of the Rules) which says that I cannot use my single sheet of paper as I see fit.

The Claims of P

The arguments of my detractors are little more than jargon strung together in phrases and sentences which superficially appear to be grammatical simply because they violate no obvious, trivial rules, and which therefore purport to have meaning. For instance, one of the most intelligent among the philosophizing Legislators, P, likes to say, "The Keeper knows no rules, he stands outside the Rules, he is *bound by no Rules*!" When I first overheard this claim, I asked myself How can the Legislator come to formulate such a claim? Upon reflection, I saw that the claim is really three claims, and that the central claim actually rests on a simple truth, the first claim is, however, a philosophical muddle, and the last claim is obviously an outright falsehood.

The separate claims (we can label them a, b, and c for simplicity in our discussion) are intended rhetorically to be identical. My detractors cheer Legislator P every time he repeats this series, which is increasingly often; indeed, they have begun to cheer at the end of each of the three separate claims in the series, cheering by far most raucously at the end of the third claim, c, which P loudly yells for extra emphasis as though it were somehow to be distinguished from the earlier claims, a and b, by virtue of its greater precision. Ironically, c is, as I have noted, the only one of the claims which is actually false. Let me briefly discuss the three claims, taking the flimsiest one first.

b: "The Keeper stands outside the Rules." Precisely. That is the philosophical definition and justification of my position. If it were not so, we would be thrown into endless circularities.

Let us consider claim c.

c: "The Keeper is bound by no Rules." The falsity of this claim is obvious, because many of the Rules have as their express object the purpose of drawing extraordinarily narrow and precise boundaries around the person and institution of the Keeper. Need one dwell on the fact of my total isolation, the strictures on my supply of paper, the removal of the Rules from my Quarters? Even my dress is prescribed in the Rules of State, I must wear these heavy robes despite the fact that no one other than my eventual apprentice will ever see me clothed as Keeper of the Rules.

Finally, let us turn to claim a, which is philosophically the most complex of P's three claims.

a: "The Keeper knows no rules." This claim is too obviously wrong for it to be taken literally, since if I knew no rules, I could form no sentences. Hence, the "claim" as stated is unquestionably in need of editing, indeed of "heavy editing," as dear P would say. I submit that the claim is a glib restatement of another claim often voiced by other Legislators. This other claim is that I cannot know that I know the rules of syntax, because if I should forget one of the rules, I would have no means of checking whether I was editing correctly. "The rules of syntax are not even written down," one of my detractors laments. "How does the Keeper even know that he knows them?" Just such rhetoric illustrates the emptiness of their philosophy. That a Keeper of the Rules cannot know that he knows! One cannot imagine that any of these "philosophers" would allow the same assertion to be made about himself. I would yell, "Legislator P, how do you know that you know the living language?" No—one need not treat their arguments seriously, and so long as I am Keeper, the Rules of State will be protected against their onslaughts.

It may have been noticed in the above discussion that I only heard these claims, a, b, and c, being made—I did not see them in writing. Therefore, I cannot know whether P intended to be saying, for instance, "The Keeper knows no rules," rather than "The Keeper knows no Rules." One cannot distinguish capital R from lower case r in the spoken word. True. If P meant the second formulation (let us designate it as a_2) instead of the first (a_1). I can only say, "But Legislator P, your claim is a platitude. After all, it was the Legislators who voted the edict that the Rules be removed from my Quarters, and it was their purpose in so doing to prevent the Keeper from knowing the Rules, dear P." Similarly, claim b may have been intended with a lower case "rules"—"The Keeper stands outside the rules." In this case the claim would be senseless rather than true—again I give P the benefit of doubt and assume that he meant the claim to be the true form. Claim c would be false in either case, as I have shown for "Rules" and as must be obvious for "The Keeper is bound by no rules."

So much for the claims of P.

I do not deny in these arguments a substantial degree of sophistication. Not all of the Legislators are competent to comprehend the debates initiated by my detractors (although many who do not comprehend these debates nonetheless judge themselves to be qualified to vote for edicts whose purpose is to circumscribe my function—so low has the quality of the Legislators fallen), and even I have on occasion had to ponder their arguments at some length in order to perceive clearly the errors implicit in them. If one did not suspect them to be somewhat ill-intentioned, one would probably expect my detractors, almost all of whom are young, to become outstanding Legislators. And perhaps their motives are not so bad as I sometimes think; perhaps they are misled more by youth than vice; perhaps they will mature past their present views against the institution of a Keeper of the Rules. This is my ardent hope. Yet I have doubts—perhaps it is inherent in one whose daily task it is to correct abundant error that he must doubt that error will disappear, as it were, of its own accord.

Choosing the Apprentice

It appears that Keepers of the Rules have all had extraordinary powers of memory, in fact I know an enormous number of the Rules of State, indeed verbatim. Likewise, my apprentice will learn past Rules from me, and he will learn from the history and traditions of the position he will eventually fill —I daresay no one but the Keeper actually knows that history and tradition. One could, of course, reconstruct much of it by deduction from those rules which govern the institution of the Keeper just as anyone with an extraordinary intellect might well learn the rules of syntax, logic, and linguistic usage merely through long, diligent, and painful study of the Rules of State. But the tradition of the Keeper is much like the rules of syntax— the current Keeper is the embodiment of the traditions of the institution.

Therefore, although the greatest protection of the continuation of our institutions is the institutions themselves, nonetheless I would fear for our State's future if I did not have ample time to prepare my apprentice for the exacting duties which he will one day face. Unfortunately however, I do not know when my apprentice is to be selected. Indeed, I do not even know the rules governing the time of appointment of apprentices—that is one area in which my predecessor and teacher failed to give me instruction, or perhaps he did and it escaped my attention, but that is unlikely. Nor do I know how my apprentice is to be selected. It might be at the discretion of the Legislators, but that would be too clearly counter to the massive intent of the Rules to maintain separation of the Legislators from the Keeper. Probably the Governors of the Hall select the apprentice at a time clearly specified in the Rules. But I am not sure, and I fear that if there is a weakness in the institutions of our State, this might be it.

As it happens, the problem of selecting my apprentice may be far more crucial than one might think, given that I am still young (since my predecessor did not live long after my appointment as apprentice to the Keeper). However, I will have to teach my apprentice far more than any past apprentice has had to learn. Not only has the number of Rules which any Keeper should have memorized grown immensely in my time, but the sophistication of the philosophizing Legislators requires much greater sophistication in the day to day activities of the Keeper—it will take my apprentice many years to become accustomed to the arduous standards of his duties.

Beyond such natural developments, there is also the matter of teaching my apprentice the elaborate shorthand which he will need to know in order to be able to keep adequate records of the duplicities of younger Legislators. It is not unlikely that the training which an apprentice undergoes before entering the Keeper's Quarters will have seduced my apprentice into thinking it immoral for him to learn such a shorthand, not to speak of listening through the chute to the debates of the Legislators. I will have to be very careful in teaching my apprentice the necessity of such practices.

Even beyond such simple considerations of the task of teaching my apprentice what he will need to know, there is another reason for urgency in appointing him. I recently heard one of the younger Legislators murmur (though I am not absolutely certain) that "It would be easier to poison the

Keeper's food than to legislate against him." *Against* me—that is the way they speak. This is the most important reason I am anxious to begin early with my apprentice: so that he can eat first at every meal. It is not inconceivable —although I doubt that it could actually come to that—that I would have to train a second apprentice if the first should not survive.

ENVOI

I have received the order, now I am expected to obey.

There are those who order if and only if there are those who obey, if orders were not obeyed they would be mere pleas. That is their odd, indeed definitive quality. An order becomes an order only in the obeyance of it, but the act of obeying can be called obeying only because there was first an order. Vicious circle. More vicious with some orders than with others.

All this sophistry is within my head. Outside my head, I am given my orders and I obey. But my head is not wholly detached in the process, in a sense my head mediates between the ordering and the obeying. If I did not understand an order, I would not obey. Not knowingly at least, which is to say, not. To understand an order is also to understand that it is an order.

I understand the order which I am given. Within my head now I only wonder, Can I not obey while nonetheless understanding my order and doing that which I am ordered to do? Could it not be mere chance and not an act of obeying that I do what I am ordered to do?

I refuse to obey my order, though I put my head in their noose, which as it happens is what they command. I refuse to be hanged even while the priest blesses me. They plead with me. I who will not obey cannot be ordered—my head is wholly detached in the process.

II

HATRED IS A SIMPLE MATTER

Hatred is a simple matter—it takes very little to explain it. For instance, his eyes—his eyes are that ugly green color that is really not green at all, that I find so repulsive. And that is a remarkable fact, because I would perhaps never have noticed the color of his eyes if I had not already suffered such an intense reaction to him, but as it happens (I am tempted to say as it *must* happen) his eyes only add to my total picture of him. And yet, I cannot say that the green color of his eyes would always evoke revulsion, because I would find, say, a leaf not displeasing even if it were that peculiar color. So it seems that this particular green gets its character in part from that which is colored with it.

His eyes contribute to the general impression of his face, as of course they must, eyes being perhaps the most outstanding feature of most faces. However, his face is such that attractive eyes would be inadequate to salvage the whole, so disagreeable is it. Although it is not essentially different from hundreds of other faces—the eyebrow which arches occasionally, the smile which wants to turn down, the nostrils which flare, German fashion, to indicate emotion, the hairline which dips lower in the middle—despite its not uncommon features, it is profoundly revolting. Why it should be so I cannot say, but when I mention my reactions to friends, even to mutual friends, they are not surprised at what I say. They can understand the sensibility which underlies my feelings. Occasionally, one of them will say, "But his lips are not different from thousands of others," or, "Yes, but there is really nothing peculiarly different about him." I agree, no single characteristic is peculiar, wrong, or even, I would almost grant, distasteful. But they are all together, and all together they are him, and all together they arouse the strongest hatred.

But I need not dwell on superficial characteristics, although facial expressions are, it would seem to me despite what most of my friends say, genuine extensions of thoughts, of character, of personal integrity, of whatever one might wish to distinguish from the "strictly superficial." And here, I can only assert that his internal character is that which is revealed in his external features. I hardly command the vocabulary to describe this internal character—loathesome? as little used as the word is, it is used too much not to have spent its force in less worthy applications. Despicable?—the word is comic in its sound and in its commonplace usages, which are far too broad.

I once heard a French aristocrat speaking on the political changes in his country. He ate an apple by biting out large chunks. He then chewed at great length to eat away all the fruit without damaging the bits of skin, which he spat into his left hand always before taking his next bite. When he finished the apple, he stood to say that he was a man of no ill feelings— he would of course not say that he loved everyone, but he surely would never have thought he could hate anyone. And yet, when he spoke of one former schoolmate of his who had become a government minister, and who had pursued policies which affected the aristocrat in ways which he did not like, he said, "But *this man* I *hate*." He had to bring out his words with such force as to move his whole body—there are no ways to say such things.

I suppose that is as it must be—hatred is such a simple matter that it requires no elaborate vocabulary. Partly therefore, perhaps, I avoid discussing him with other people—despite the cited testimonies of friends, I have actually seldom discussed him with them. But when I do get involved in longer discussions about him, I find that many of my friends not only are not surprised at what I say, they actually agree, if not wholly, at least in large part with my view of him, although evidently no one with whom I have spoken has ever reached such conclusions altogether independently of my remarks. Of course, no one else ever quite comes to the point of hatred—rather, they all merely agree that his eyes are repulsive, that his voice defies listening, or whatever. But I suspect that if there were not strong tendencies—I would almost say "codes"—to avoid any expression of so deep and simple a feeling as hatred, they would admit to fuller agreement with my view. As it is however, these strong tendencies perhaps are so effective as to prevent their even realizing such a feeling within themselves. If this were not so, I would have to suspect them of hypocrisy, but I do not think they are genuinely hypocritical.

And even among those who do not really agree with my view of him, one can detect a sense of their suspecting that although they do not fully understnad the origin of my hatred, nonetheless they cannot quite imagine that it could be so intense and yet be wholly unfounded. Therefore, although they neither hate him nor understand why I should, they increasingly suspect that he is at least partly at fault. Indeed, since my discomfort, one could say my suffering, is so great, they tend to suspect that he is almost exclusively at fault, since I could surely not bring such pain upon myself. One might therefore think that I would at least find some comfort in their support, but I am not sure—I think it might perhaps be better if they took no note of my hatred or of him, because then they would never fall into conversation about him. It is possible in fact that their recognition of my hatred and their acceptance of its probable validity in the face of their lack of understanding presents them with a problem of such interest that they cannot refrain from discussing it in the hope of solving it. But when I overhear their discussions, however involuntarily, I recall him to my thoughts and invariably I am brought to nervous shaking, and my head is soon pounding with hatred of him. I wish I had never mentioned my hatred of him to anyone—I could almost hate myself that I have said anything about it. When others offer what they think will be soothing words, my pain is only doubled.

At the moment, the worst thing about my hatred of him, now that I have fully recognized it for what it is and have verified in him its validity, is that our town is sufficiently small that I cannot escape contact with him, hearing him, seeing him. And yet, any involvement with him, of whatever variety, gives me a headache of such severity as almost to incapacitate me, and these headaches last hours, occasionally a full day or more. When I overhear conversations about him, I frequently begin to shake at the thought of the headache which will soon come upon me. In the center of town my head will begin to throb so that my view merges into a single pulsating light, and I can find my way home only after several wrong turns. My knees finally grow so queasy that I think I must collapse before I reach my bed where, though I do not escape the pain, at least I can escape being subjected to discussions about him.

The only cure for headaches brought on by him is their very severity, for eventually they reduce me to a total incapacity even to think about him. Just this, of course, is what is needed, and after a nap or a night's sleep following on my loss of thought, the headache is almost invariably past. When it is not, I can only imagine that its continuation is to be attributed to dreams about him, although I never specifically remember such dreams. There was a time when I could cure the headaches brought on my him by merely calming myself in a rocking chair and slowly eating an apple—the munching soothed my nerves. But when the headaches became more acute, they began almost always to be accompanied by such nausea as to make eating an apple seem nearly as despicable as talking with him. Now the mere sight of an apple brings on thoughts of him and the inevitable headache. Hence he is made more odious to me by the fact that he denies me some of the usual pleasures of life—I resent him the more that he evokes such a thorough and demanding hatred.

One might suspect from the intensity of my feelings toward him that I was deeply involved with him, knew him well, lived close to him, and so on. But it is not so. I have hardly spoken with him—indeed, the sense of loathing which his voice arouses in me prevents me from speaking with him unless it is utterly unavoidable, and even then I have never let any conversation linger past the necessary amenities of Hello, How are you, Goodbye. For a long while after each such exchange, I hate myself almost as spitefully as I hate him. In each of these encounters I try to be as rude as one can possibly be while saying those things which invariably must be said in the game of meeting, saying hello, and going on quickly. Just to spite me, he forces himself to be polite and kindly in his tone, as if he really cared for my well being, despite the obvious, visible effect which he has on me, and therefore I hate his every word.

When I see him unexpectedly, and there is no way to avoid meeting, I am immediately taken with such a severe headache that I clasp my hands to my ears and, with my elbows jutting outward, squeeze my head as though to crush out its pain by blocking out his voice. My grimace would startle a less hateful person into silence, causing him to pass on quietly to remove the source of my pain. But he cannot be startled into silence no matter how rude I am, he has not the least shred of human decency, he attacks me with his repugnant voice, "Why hello! How are you?" When the dreadful moment is past and I am stumbling to make my way back home, they are already asking one another what was the occasion for my feeling ill. They wonder whether he did anything during our few seconds of meeting to upset me. "Did you hear?" "Did he say anything more than 'How are you?' " "I wish I had been closer to hear everything—what do you think it was?" But it is not one statement any more than it is merely the color of his eyes.

There have been moments lately when I have begun to imagine what my life would be like if interest in my hatred of him were to become widespread in the town. He would then have transcended himself to intrude upon me at all times from all quarters, and I would be denied thoughts of anything but him with all the physical effects which such a permanent sensation of hatred would imply. When this image comes to me, usually in the pit of headache, but occasionally in the midst of a day which has proceeded happily up until that moment, then I am almost debilitated, my hatred is multiplied, I think how cruel he is to pursue me so viciously for no evident reason, for no profit. Were I not so incapacitated by his presence, I would instantly seek him out to ask him *Why? What do you have against me?* I wish only that I could overcome my physical involvement with hatred long enough to approach him, to demand full answers from him. Does he think I really deserve such bestial treatment? Had I only imagined years ago that his presence would become so insidious for me, I might have addressed him with my questions. But now that would be impossible for me to bear—and now the community addresses *me.*

Many of my friends and my family suggest to me that it is not a healthy thing to indulge such a strong feeling of hatred —they do not say it explicitly, but one can sense that, in so many words, this is the essence of what they wish to impress upon me. And I agree with them. Life becomes increasingly difficult for me, so that now even when I have not seen him for many days, I am still unable to keep myself from lapsing into periods, often into extended periods, of dwelling on my hatred of him, so that I suffer from almost constant headache. I can picture his features in my mind more clearly than I can envision my own features or those of my family. But there seems to be no way for me to overcome my hatred no matter how diligently I work at it—I have no means of driving him from our community. He is destroying my existence. That fact alone renews and reinforces my hatred of him.

BLOCKED VIEW

I looked back quickly, but the trees and bushes blocked my view so that I could make out nothing, at least while running. While turning my head I nearly stumbled, but I caught my balance by grabbing a limb. I was approaching a fence line not far ahead. I veered slightly to the left, ran along the fence for a short distance, finally stopped beside a post, and clambered up and over. On the other side I was soon out of the trees, but the terrain was much rougher, so that still I could not see very far around myself in any direction. There were shallow ditches—perhaps from erosion—which made progress clumsy and treacherous. I was frequently stumbling and coming down on all fours, but since the ditches were invariably at the lowest points between the ridges, I came down headed uphill and did not sprawl so badly as I might have expected, and I was always aimed so that I could instantly regain momentum. Over the top of the last of the ridges, I headed down into a field of high grass. I had not thought to look back while at the crest of the ridge, and now again the view was blocked. I came out of the grass to stumble into a ditch running beside a narrow roadway, jumped back to my feet and trotted down the road for several yards before crossing it to enter the field on the other side. The field cleared before a house, a small wood frame house which looked more like a holiday home than a farm, and which appeared at a glance to be boarded up. However, I did not stop to make sure of that, but ran for a small clump of trees, and there paused to catch breath. Again, I could not see clearly enough to see where I had just come from or where I might go. My view was at every moment limited to a narrow patch—of terrain, brush, trees, sky. Relationships and connections were missing. The sky was the only constant, although it was the one part of the view which I seldom noted—it did not impede my progress. Only while stopped for a few minutes could I even reflect on the sky as part of the view, perhaps only now when all else was stationary did the sky betray a sense of movement. Could the sky be moving? What would that mean? If there had been birds perhaps, but there were no birds—there had been no life along my path, insects probably and of course plants, but nothing more that I could remember. On a glance around I noticed that everything else was now moving, there must have been a slight breeze, now only I was stationary and perhaps the ground. Watching the trees shivering, I began to think that pausing had been a mistake, because I could now feel my legs throbbing as though to mock the trees. My chest was heaving, but the more air I gulped to soothe it, the more it ached. For a fleeting moment I even felt I would faint, or at least that my body would lose consciousness even if my mind did not. That was odd, because I had developed a headache which could only have been described as a sick headache, as though my head were nauseated. Relationships between my various parts were becoming confused. When I began to think that it was impossible to run any further, I realized that it was time to get back into motion. At first I waved my arms around myself to loosen joints which had congealed in rebellion, and then I ran in place for a moment, and, without a specific action to change position, I was underway again. The terrain here was easy for running but the tall field grass slashed at my arms, occasionally even my face. Perhaps that was a good combination—I could move without too great exertion on my legs as they accustomed themselves again to running, and the irritation of the grass kept my mind off my pains without seriously impeding my progress. Soon the grass thinned out and was gone. I ran until I felt the ground falling out from under me, turned briefly to look back, noticed that I was on a downhill, and then slowed from a run to a fast walk, occasionally skipping, and even running. There were shabby bushes at what seemed to be the bottom of the slope, and I found myself slipping in the loose soil and sliding into the bushes face first. Instinct closed my eyes and opened my hands to catch my fall. I rolled enough to cover my sweat-soaked clothes and body with dirty soil and sand mingled with humus. I sat for a moment to rub my arms clean—it was no use, so I was back to my feet and prying my way through the bushes. By the time the bushes cleared, soil had given way to sand, and I was clambering uphill. Although my muscles were now running again, my body was hardly making progress because my feet gained no hold in the sand. It seemed much more enervating to run now than it had before, and I made much less headway for my effort. Again it was uphill and down—this time over sand dunes. And again I could see little distance when I tried to look back. There was water in the air, I could taste it—as though it were approaching from above, having already surrounded and cooled my head without yet reaching my tired feet. I struggled over several dunes, could now see nothing but sand in any direction, but smelled water ever richer. I was already running-slipping down the last of the dunes before my sweat bleared eyes brought the green water into focus. Now I could see farther than at any time in the last few hours, but only before me, not behind. The running was easier now, where the ground was even so that I did not have to contend with slopes, and where, because it was moist, the sand was stiffer. I was running along the shore—the sand was now wet and hard—I was even sometimes splashing through the water's shallow indentations into the shore. I turned to look over my shoulder once more, but now my vision was so blurred with sweat and tears that I could hardly distinguish the dunes, which must, in any case, have blocked any farther view. I was stumbling into the water and splashing myself up into the face. I fell forward and began half to swim and half to kick the bottom. Finally I was swimming fully, at first erratically, but then more evenly so that my only sensation was of steady motion and rhythmic splashing noises. The only interruption of my smooth progress was when I occasionally broke stroke to look back over my shoulder. But the undulating water blocked my view, which had now become identical in all directions.

III

A BEGINNING

The letter said that as soon as I could manage to bring my things down to show them, they would likely be prepared to give me a position to support my work. I was very pleased, pleasure was only natural, one does not often receive such encouraging invitations, one has lost hope at my age. Suddenly I was beginning to feel like a new beginning, never again to fear that I should not be able to continue my work, were I the kind, I would have sung.

If I were to receive the position, I would have to move down to the City, the City was far away, it would be both a long and big move. That prospect necessitated at least a little planning, singing could wait, I had never made such a major move, I had not even left my parents' house, they had left mine. But out of the past into the future—planning—I had at all events to be careful to keep my work together. It seemed wise to prepare all my things for a quick move in the event I got the position and to arrange all my work separate from the other things so that I could take all of it, the work, or at least the better part of it, on the first trip down to the City when I would be talking to them the first time. That was of course the best way to pack everything anyway, so that it would not be a very great chore. Oh it would be a great chore to pack, but not a great chore to keep the work separate from the other things, given that I would be packing everything in one way or another in any event.

Oh me, I bore even me whose life it is, that is the price of clarity, I apologize, but it was clarity in my work got me the letter in the first place, I cannot readily give it up merely for the telling of the tale, but I had to pack.

First however I should answer their letter, I went down to reheat coffee to think out my answering letter, the coffee was left over from many days before, it smelled revolting, I drank it quickly so as not to have to smell it too long. I could not remember when last I had written a letter, I looked for paper, for pen, for envelopes, for stamps, I had none of them, oh paper of course, but not such as would be fit for a letter. I went down to my bicycle to ride into Town to fetch the things I needed. The bicycle had a flat tire, details aside, to repair the tire required the remainder of the day.

The following day I prepared again to go into Town, it was too nice for cycling, I walked. The way is not so long, there are shortcuts, there is joy in cutting the world short. I took my cane, I took my hat, I took my case, and I betook me to the road. The road here is dirt which means that sometimes it is mud, sometimes dust, that day it was dust, when a vehicle passed, I was dust, shortly I took to the fields, shortly the fields turned to woods.

The woods were more interesting, less hot, but they are included in none of the shortcuts. In mid afternoon I turned back for home to rest the night. Next day I rode the bicycle to Town and bought paper, pen, envelopes, but no stamps, it was Saturday, the post office was closed. No matter, I had Sunday to write my letter, Monday I could go to Town to mail it, Tuesday I could begin to pack.

Forgive me, I return to boring us for a moment, packing must be planned, it would be disastrous to arrive in the City without some part of my work which I had overlooked and left behind, thence to fail to get the position only because the mood of the meeting had not been quite right. Perhaps that one missing part of my work would have added just the slight weight to shift opinion positively into my favor. I would never know whether that bit of my work would have made the difference, I would be in doubt even about the justice of castigating myself for the oversight of leaving it behind, in the matter of moods one can never be quite sure what it is that changes joy to despair, favor to disfavor. Clearly I could not be too careful in planning the things to be taken on the first trip down, although disfavor might as readily attend too great care as too little.

I divided my things into two piles—my work and all the other things. Perfect. Now for packing what more did I need, sacks perhaps, yes, many sacks.

Back to Town for sacks, I looked for the bicycle, where could it have gone, oh yes of course, into the pile of other things. On the morrow I rode the cycle to Town for sacks in which to pack my work. One senses more clearly the need for clarity, not merely in my work but in my planning as well, singing could be reserved for long hours on the bicycle.

The sacks did not work well, especially not for heavy things, for gangly things, for large things, all my things it seemed were heavy, gangly, sometimes large. The next week I tried boxes, they worked better, a week later crates worked better still, all my things were packed in crates, a stack of crates to the left for all my work, a stack of crates to the right for all the other things, unless one looked from behind when the former was on the right, the latter on the left. I was ready for an immediate move, I decided it was time to take my work down to show them and to ask for my position.

I had to go to the City.

How should I get there, not how should I get there, but how should I get there with all the crates of my work? Yes, how. Well. I was tired from packing the crates, I slept, I slept the whole night, thence the whole day, not often do I sleep the whole day, only when I face a tedious decision, perhaps dreaming gives answers, the solution to the problem of life it is said is found when the problem disappears, my problems disappear in a deep slumber, I found the solution to my problem—buy a car.

I slept another night and rose early to walk to Town. Walk? Yes, if I bought a car, I would not wish to leave my cycle in the town. I found a car, it cost too much, they would let me pay by installment, I would earn the installments if I got the position which I could get only if I had the car to take my work and me to the City, one perceives an element of circularity there, oh me.

I found on driving home that the car was not made for shortcuts, it lodged overnight in a field, the farmer nearly shot me before he towed me out next morning, I then took the long road, which is the road, home. Details, blithering details.

The crates were too big to fit in the car. I slept two days, took the car back to Town, traded it for a van with bigger installment payments, the crates fit in the van. I slept three days more, it might be easier I thought if I never woke. Somniferous clarity.

The further I go, the more the details seem, I could not find the letter with the address of my benefactor, where did it go, perhaps in one of the crates of my work, I decrated my work, one crate after the other, no letter, the van stood empty. A week passed, I decrated my other things, no letter, the dealer came for the first installment, I had as yet no money from my position, he wanted money. I tried to explain. One should not see the world as a set of unconnected facts, true enough it was a fact I had no money for his installment, still one must look further, such facts often have reasons. "My money," he said, he insisted on the facts, he wanted no reasons, he took instead the empty van, I slept two weeks.

I was now in a quandary, I reviewed the past weeks in the hope of introducing still greater clarity into my further planning. It was time to begin again, not in order to begin but in order to again, I know, grammar does not allow it, but.

I slept another night, another day, another night, I got up to ride my cycle down to the City to look for benefactors who might have made me an offer to support my work, yes, it would be many days' ride, no matter, I had slept long and well slumbering for a solution to my problem, at last I had long hours on the bicycle in which to sing for joy that I had received such an encouraging invitation, and peddling, trying to escape the dust I raised, peddling with the energy of a new beginning, I sang and sang and sang.

POETS' PARTY

The earliest known entry in my family tree was a poet. Although he was not the greatest poet of his age, he was widely read and respected—on occasion he was even invited to read at court. His last poem describes his "good and pleasant life." Since then, many have studied his poetry, and there are not a few scholars who consider themselves experts on his life and work.

I, too, am a poet. But now life is different. No one reads me, I am nearly unknown beyond the local community of poets. And even among them, I am only recently known.

Not long ago I mentioned to one of my neighbors that I am a poet. "You are?" he said. "I never would have guessed. I heard you had an ancestor who was a poet, but you ..." He was shaking his head, "I'm a poet too."

"You are?" I said, and it was only with some effort that I kept from repeating his "I never would have guessed." We were understandably startled—although neither of us knew many other poets, there we were, two in the same building.

When I was younger, I wondered—Could I be such a bad poet? But now there can be no question, the poetry which I write is superior to that of my ancestor. "Oh?" you ask, "then why is it not more widely read?" A difficult question. Modern critics are generally agreed that the principle according to which my ancestor wrote was a simple one. Namely, there is only one right way of persuading: that is to present what is true in such a way that nothing will prevent the reader from seeing it except the desire to remain unenlightened. Now the modern reader need not be very sophisticated to recognize this premise as quaint. Nonetheless, he will expect to hear reasons why I think I am a better poet than my ancestor only to be less well read.

Unfortunately, I cannot clearly state any such reasons, although I am sure there are reasons, indeed reasons which have little to do with me or my poetry. And I am not the only person who thinks so—my view is shared by many others who have given long years of thought to the problem. After we each discovered that the other was a poet, my neighbor and I discussed the problem at great length. He suggested that we hold a party, an evening of discussion and wine. We would ask our poet friends to ask their poet friends, who in turn should ask their poet friends, and so forth.

From our building there were eight poets at the party. From this single block there were seventy-three poets. Among us we could think of another twenty-three poets living on the block who did not come to the party. Before the party I had known only three of these ninety-six people as poets, and had known perhaps another dozen without knowing they were poets.

We had to send out for more wine. My neighbor's apartment was somewhat crowded—when I wanted to go to the toilet at one point, I had first to ask the eleven poets and poetesses gathered in there to please stand outside for a minute. We enjoyed the party so much that most of us stayed all night, and in the morning we sent out for fifteen dozen eggs and six loaves of bread to make breakfast. Naturally, one finds pleasure in knowing others who share his interests.

But after the evening of the poets' party I became somewhat depressed. And my depression deepened each time I read at length the poetry of any of these other poets, as I have been doing now that I know them and know that I can so conveniently meet with them.

Actually, that is not strictly true, because when I read the poetry of the first two or three of them, I was very much elated—their work was extraordinarily good. But then I kept finding the work of almost every one of my fellow neighborhood poets extraordinarily good. There must be several dozen unusually fine poets living on this single block alone.

When we discovered how talented we all are, most of us went in together to buy a mimeograph machine. We now prepare mimeographs of any new poems we write in order to exchange current work with our fellow neighborhood poets. I am not sure, but I suspect that mutual encouragement has stimulated all of us to write more than ever, better than ever. My desk drawers have filled with thousands of mimeographed poems—I no longer manage to file the copies by poets' names. We have had to hire someone to run our mimeograph machine and to distribute the copies to us, and he seems to be lagging several days behind. Next week we will probably hire a part time assistant for him.

Every day I receive nearly a hundred new poems, and if I were to read all of them, I would hardly have time to write one myself. Yet, almost all of the ones I read seem to be exceptionally well done—there is so much to be learned from that I should be reading them far more carefully.

My own work has been heavily influenced by my fellow neighborhood poets. My poetry has improved so dramatically that yesterday I threw away all poems which I wrote before this year. My depression has now turned to elation—I think I cannot fail to gain a wider audience soon. My ancestor would envy his descendant.

THE HOME OFFICE

I work as hard as other people, only that I work at home. This has presented problems more or less from the beginning, but my way of life grows increasingly difficult, I am not sure that I can continue to withstand the censures of my fellow tenants.

My working here should disturb no one. I keep regular hours, that is to say I sleep when others sleep. I am quiet, my work is desk work (one would call me an office worker except that, as is known, I work at home). My constant presence here should comfort those who worry about burglars. In short, I am the ideal fellow tenant, not least *because* I work at home. Why should the other tenants object?

When I go down to check the four o'clock mail, I frequently meet other tenants as they are returning home from work. Needless to say, I, too, have put in a day's work by then. Indeed, I have probably worked longer than they have—not requiring a long journey to get to work (that is one of the great advantages of working at home), I am already hard at work long before they have arrived at the places of their jobs. Similarly, I have been continuously at work until the minute before I stand at my mailbox, whereas they have long since ended their efforts for the day. Yet *they* scorn *me*.

Today at the mailbox Mrs. Richards asked me, "What are you doing these days?"

"Oh, working very hard," I said. Did she believe me? I don't think she did.

Why should she not believe me?

After collecting her mail, without another word to me, she went back up to her rooms, no doubt to relax for the remainder of the day before retiring early to bed. Whereas I, when I went back up to my rooms, it was to continue working until late in the evening. My labors are hardly interrupted even by meals.

But Mrs. Richards is not the worst. I seldom encounter her, and the rudest thing she ever says is "What are you doing these days?" No, her interrogations I could withstand easily, if it were not for the others, such as Mrs. Bamberg, the superintendent's wife, who seems always to be lurking there, although she works at a store far away. She came up to me today just after Mrs. Richards had gone up the stairs.

"Hello, Mr. Hard-Worker, how are you today?" she asked. She must have overheard my conversation with Mrs. Richards.

"Tired," I answered, "very tired—other than that quite all right, thank you. And you?"

"Me?" she asked. "Why should I be tired? I only work for a living."

Was she trying to insult me? She who would spend the rest of the afternoon in her great easy chair nodding herself half to sleep, she should insult *me*? Besides, how could she know that I spent the whole day in my rooms? And even if she knew that, which is out of the question, still she could not "know" that I was not hard at work there at every moment. By facile deduction she presumes to know that I do not work as hard as she does.

The frequency and intensity of the insults have begun to upset my work and my life—some days I am almost reluctant to go to fetch my mail. On occasion I am so intimidated that I descend by the fire escape with my briefcase in hand in order to be able, then, to enter the front door as though returning home from work. Maybe someone has seen me.

I think perhaps I should go back to the more common life style, perhaps I should return to working in my office. I have thought of it for a long while, I would have done it already, only that I am worried about the reaction of my fellow office workers. For instance, on my occasional visits to the office, one of the secretaries almost invariably greets me with, "Why hello sir. Have you come to get supplies?"

I have never yet devised an answer, I merely fill my briefcase as quickly as possible and return home to work. It is not that I am embarrassed, I have no reason to be embarrassed, I work as hard as they do. No, it is simply that they think I must be embarrassed, they think if I do not work in the office, I do not work, therefore they treat me as though I were embarrassed.

Their treatment of me becomes a source of embarrassment to us all.

MY WINDOW

Yesterday my window moved.

It used to be at the center of the wall, so that I could look out past the building next door into the park. Not that the park was terribly beautiful—it had deteriorated badly in recent years—but it did have trees. But now the window is in the far corner, there, partly hidden behind the bookcase. Because of the bookcase, I can see out the window only from this sharp angle, and I can no longer see the park but can only see into the window of the apartment in the building next door.

Needless to say, it is gloomy here now that the window has moved. To look from one dingy window to another. Never again to see trees?

In the park on occasion I used to see birds. Although the trees are not as healthy as they once were, their blooms were still a pleasure last spring. One moonlit night not long ago, I saw two lovers—they must have been teenagers with no other place to do it. I suspect they would not even have minded that I watched. But now my park might just as well have gone, they could be constructing on it for all I know.

This morning I reported the moving of my window to the maid.

"No, no, Mr. Jones," she said, without so much as a glance at the window. "I'm sure it's always been right there where it is. I swear, you're working too hard, Mr. Jones, you look fevered. I'll make the bed, and then you can lie down. Come, come . . ."

I am not Mr. Jones, of course, nor was I Mr. Smith last week, nor Mr. Black before that. Nor will I be Mr. Whatever next week. And the window has moved.

I called the rental agency this afternoon. The woman who answered the phone said, "I beg your pardon."

"I said my window has moved and I would like to have it moved back where it was."

"Windows *don't* move."

"I know. But it did."

"I'm sorry sir."

She wanted to end the conversation. I asked to speak with her supervisor.

"I don't have a supervisor, sir."

"You have to have a supervisor. It's in the regulations."

After a short pause, in a much quieter voice, she said, "Yes sir. One moment please."

Her supervisor said it too, "Windows *don't* move."

I began to feel like Galileo at the Inquisition. "Nevertheless," I said, "it has moved." I was allowed to speak with the director of the agency.

The director was very gracious. He seemed to understand my problem with the woman and her supervisor. After a brief conversation, he switched me back to the woman with whom I had originally spoken.

She was now contrite. "Let's see, sir, what was it you said? Your window has moved?"

"Yes, that's right. And I would like to have it moved back."

"Yes. Well, it may be difficult. First we'll have to send a man to check it. It may be a few days though—we don't have anyone on windows. It's not a common complaint, as you might imagine. We'll have to make a special arrangement. We'll call you when we have someone. Will that be all right?"

"Yes—that will be fine. Thank you."

"And thank you for calling. Please call us whenever you need anything."

It has been a few days now.

I wonder whether they will fix it—she didn't want to send a man. After all, windows don't move. In the meantime I must do without my view of the park.

I suppose I will have to settle for looking into the apartment next door. It is not entirely uninteresting, and with my lights off they cannot tell that I am watching them.

The gloom is beginning to lift somewhat. Perhaps I can get used to no trees. It could be worse—the park might never have been there in the first place. Or the window might not merely have moved, it might have disappeared altogether. Indeed, there need never have been a window at all.

It might move back.

A PECULIAR BEHAVIOR

I have been noticing lately a certain peculiar behavior. My train will come into the station, and while it waits there with its doors open, another passenger across the aisle from me, beside me, or perhaps at the other end of the car will sit calmly looking at the sign which names the station, and then after the train has waited a minute and only shortly before the train leaves the station, the other passenger makes a sudden dash out of the train just as its doors close. Of course, everyone has witnessed such scenes on occasion—perhaps the other passenger was lost in faraway thoughts, only looking in the direction of the station sign but not really looking at it, and came to his senses only in the last moment before the train would have gone on to carry him past his station. I am sure that I have seen such things in past years and only have not remembered them because the explanation was so clear. But now that explanation will no longer suffice—this peculiar behavior is no longer a random rare occurrence, it is becoming almost the order of the day.

Indeed, it is now commonplace that, while my train is waiting in a station, a passenger—I use the word in a very broad sense—enters alone, casually seats himself, and then suddenly exits again just before the doors close for the train to leave. All in the same station. Now the old explanation cannot possibly apply. Surely the people who behave in such a fashion know what station they are in—it is not simply the case that they discover it only after entering my train. Perhaps one would argue, "Yes, they know, but they know it better after entering the train." No, one could just as well suppose that I could enter a subway thinking vaguely that I was not comfortable, and that I meet an acquaintance in the train who says, "Oh, you have a headache!" and I respond, "Yes, that's right, isn't it—I'm sorry, I can't talk any longer just now, I now know better that my head aches, I must go back home, take some aspirin and lie down for a while," and I quickly leave the train just before its doors close and it pulls out of the station. Absolutely not—this scene is inconceivable. And yet not infrequently I see another passenger sitting in my car as we—I should perhaps say only "I"—wait for the train to leave, and he waits too long, jumps to the door as it is closing, tries to hold it open, fails, shrugs his shoulders as the train starts out of the station, returns to his seat, and waits several stations before finally getting off, as though he had to build up energy to make a new attempt.

Recently, all other passengers rose and, after fixing their eyes on me for a brief moment, fled from the car at the last second while I sat there alone, watching them climb the stairs out of the station as the train and I continued on our way. Why should they have stared at me?

LOOSE PIGS

"The pigs have broken loose!"

"Huh?"

"The pigs, the pigs, the goddamn pigs have broken loose."

"Oh," I understood. The natives called them hogs—hogs, sows, swine, they were all pigs to us, how many?, forty, four hundred, four thousand, more yet, who knows, they were loose, the goddamn pigs were loose and we were running, we were running, shit, we ran, the pigs behind us, the pigs loose.

I saw Mary, I yelled, "Run, Mary, goddamn it, run, the pigs are loose!" She ran, she asked "Why?" Did she understand? I don't know, she ran, oh god, the goddamn pigs, I heard them snorting, I swear I could hear the goddamn pigs snorting, farting, loose pigs, four thousand is not half enough, it might be forty thousand, run, goddamn, run, run, we ran, pigs ran, we all ran because the pigs ran, we prayed they wouldn't roll, my god, forty thousand rolling rooting pigs, we'd be reduced to truffles in their wake, don't roll pigs, don't don't don't, the way not to roll is stay on your feet, Mary rolled, I rolled, we had set a bad example, and then we were up and running again, the pigs closer, we could smell the farts of the farting pigs. "I'm tired," Mary said. "Oh my god, don't be tired now, not now not now not now, run, the pigs are closing in." "But I *am* tired, now now now, ohhhhh, I hate pigs." The lead pig was between us now and when I reached out to take her hand,

Mary's hand, the lead pig pushed her aside, she stumbled, rolled, and came up sitting astride the lead pig. The pig farted, glanced at me, and turned on his speed, I was chasing one pig, four million pigs were chasing me, "Charlie, that pig's got Mary, Charlie, that pig's got Mary." "Goddamn oh goddamn." The pigs were all around us, we were running with the pigs, with the pigs we ran, they led the way and at the front the the lead pig had Mary on his back, the farting all around made me dizzy, I no longer saw Mary, just pigs, forty million goddamn pigs. At the bottom of the hill we turned to follow the valley, the hill was pink with pigs behind us, the bushes were gone, the tents were down, the pigs had made way, and now the valley had its turn. The first of the campers saw us, "Oh my god," and ran for the trees, in half a minute forty campers climbed trees, another half minute the pigs destroyed the camp, Mary's pig leading the way, now I was tired, I wanted to ride, I stumbled and rode, "It's easier to ride, Charlie, why don't you ride," Charlie rode too, four hundred million goddamn pigs around us, pigs as far as we could see behind us, Charlie and I were riding, Mary was leading the way, the pigs were farting, before us at the bottom of the valley was the first town.

ART OF PERFECT FUGUE

A great symmetrical ear it was, with the organ centered at the narrowest part of the building, with acoustical ceilings suspended like hollowed out *Brötchen* at either side for the organist to spread his music upon. Perfect. The sound was integrated electronically at almost every point in the two halves of the hall to give perfect reproduction of the sounds of the most perfectly engineered organ ever. Hans would practice for several weeks just to be prepared perfectly to locate the keys, stops, and pedals of the great organ. However, to retain the moment of perfection at its most perfectly savorable flavor, he would practice not at the organ itself, but at his keyboard and pedal replica without pipes.

He had tried every organ of repute on the search for perfection in playing Bach. Every time he had been sorely disappointed: in Aachen that upper C# pipe was wrong. In Köln all of the largest set of pipes, or rather all of the set of largest pipes, were wrong. In Basel it was the clumsy pedals. In Winchester it was simply the whole cathedral which was wrong. He had gone nearly everywhere. To Ulm where the stops were so stiff, especially in the winter. And to Strasbourg—ach! that bay, that horrid bay in Strasbourg. In frustration he had even gone to Augsburg. To Augsburg! What a low estate. But as it must be, the search was futile. He had had to come to America to have the perfect organ and the perfect organ house built.

For that he had been born, for that he had lived. His mother had borne and reared *Kinder wie die Orgelpfeife*—children like the organ pipes in perfectly descending gradations of height. But then, in the fifteenth year she had missed, and the fifteenth child had been born in the place of what should have been the sixteenth and there must forever be a missing pipe in the *Kinderreihe,* in the row of children, *Kinder wie die Orgelpfeife.* Hans had never quite forgiven his father for being ill in the fifteenth year.

But, as an organ pipe child, Hans had dedicated himself at an early age to the organ. He, like Mozart, was a child prodigy, but his was a different prodigious task—his was to master the organ, not the piano and not composition, for after all the greatest organ music had already been written, and the greatest age for composing organ music was long past and never more to return. The tinsel world could never produce the harmony of life that was Bach's. And now—*die Flitterwelt.* Such irony, that the perfect organ music was written in an age of harmony but could only be perfectly played in an age of tinsel, of *Flitter. Amerika, die Flitterwelt.* Hans Strobel, Herr Orgel-meister Strobel, came to America where the perfect organ in the perfect organ hall was being built for him to play Bach to perfection.

In his childhood the other children had teased him:
> *Ich kenne doch den Apfelstrudel,*
> *Aber was ist bloss ein Hansel Strudel?*

"I am familiar with the applestrudel, but what can be a Hansel Strudel?" They were wrong of course: it was not Strudel, it was Strobel, the future Herr Orgelmeister Strobel. But they were always wrong.

In Aachen, for instance, they had told him there was a perfect organ. For he began his professional playing in Aachen, where, they all said, there was such a magnificent instrument.

An instrument they dared call it! It was no instrument, it was an organ. Moreover, they were wrong—it was not perfect, the C# pipe up high was wrong. The C#pipe. He had grown to hate Aachen. Once he left, he determined never to return—the dissonant memory of that C#. It always came in, failed to come in, half-failed to come and half-came in, at the most excruciating moment in the two mirror fugues. Most organists avoided the two mirror fugues because it is almost impossible to play them convincingly on one instrument—on one organ. But not Hans. And only to have that *Teufelswerk* C# pipe spoil it all.

The C# pipe ruined the Art of Fugue, the Art of Fugue! which was a sum of contrapuntal knowledge and which should only be played perfectly.

During his two years in Aachen, Hans had learned to flinch when he knew that the C# pipe must be played. It was always agony to know that it must come and to be able to do nothing about it. And he had begun to dream of having a perfect organ, one on which the C# pipe was not wrong. *"Das wäre was,"* he would mutter as the C# was past, "That would be something." But in Aachen there was no hope. The pipe would have to be replaced, and the repair would have to be cleared through the bishop. The new pipe would have to look like the others, which was out of the question, since such pipes were no longer made, at least not since 1792. And given a choice between looking right and sounding right, the bishop would choose looking right every time. For after all, the instrument—*"ORGEL! Orgel, sagt man."*—was played only occasionally, but it was seen daily by the hordes of rich American tourists who left offerings on the basis of what they saw, not of what they heard—even if they were to hear, surely no one would expect Americans to be able to tell the difference anyway. Especially if the Germans could not even tell.

So Hans had left Aachen to begin what became a tour of the best organs in Germany and hence in Europe. In the end he had come to *Amerika. Die Flitterwelt mit perfekter Orgel.*

Aachen however had taught him a great lesson. In Aachen Hans had been forced to have a keyboard and pedal replica of the Aachener Organ built for his practice sessions—only by practicing without the intrusion of dissonant notes from the imperfect pipe could he achieve the perfection in his play which permitted his performance to be as nearly perfect as the imperfect C# pipe allowed. In retrospect that became a boon to him, for now he could practice his playing on a replica of the perfect keyboard, pedals, and stops of the new American organ without having to hear the sounds until indeed he had made their production a perfect process.

In the papers the announcement said merely:

HANS STROBEL
THE ART OF FUGUE
J.S. BACH

But Hans knew that it was to be "The Art of Perfect Fugue," and in his grander moments he preferred "The Perfect Art of Fugue," or in all fairness to Bach, he thought the best characterization would be "The Perfect Art of Perfect Fugue." But this was America, and they would not understand.

The debut of Hans Strobel, Deutscher Orgelmeister, was enough to guarantee a sell-out for the first performance ever in the new organ hall on the new organ.

Even the lighting was extraordinary—Hans fairly glowed in the center of the hall at the narrowest point with the two acoustic ceilings suspended to either side of him. He bowed with crisp perfection, the applause engulfed him from acoustically superb directions. He turned, paused, sat, put aside the notes in a gesture of perfect conceit, raised his arms—and then!

The sound was stupendous as in the first fugue Hans treated the main subject in a simple manner. He then paused unduly long without acknowledging the presence of the audience. Then in the second fugue he treated the main subject again in a simple manner, but counterpointed with a dotted rhythm. At the end of the second fugue, again he paused, though now in consternation. Then reluctantly he played the third fugue on the inverted subject with a chromatic counter-subject and with its exquisite middle section in which the inverted subject appears a little ornamented and, of course, in syncopation. By now there was no gainsaying—it was wrong.

Hans stood: "It is not perfect. It is wrong. It is wrong!" His voice was under perfect control, clipped and precise, and because the acoustics were so good, his words were audible throughout the hall. Once more he declared, "It is wrong," and then he stalked perfectly, precisely out of the hall, still four fugues before the intermission.

Hans accused the manager of the hall of treason against music for having misrepresented the by now clearly un-perfect organ. Yes, the manager had noticed that it was not so perfect—"so *nearly* perfect," Hans corrected—yes, it was not so nearly perfect as he had thought. But he would have it checked and reset, perfectly.

"They are incompetent, they are all incompetent," Hans muttered as he parted.

Electronic experts came with all their paraphernalia, their db-meters and oscilloscopes. They checked, checked, and re-checked the perfect organ, and (they insisted), found it perfect. The manager called Hans to tell him.

In a few minutes Hans stood before the manager.

"What is it, Herr Strobel?"

"Whether you plan to correct it," he ordered. "*That* I wish to know."

The manager tried again and again to tell Hans that the

organ was indeed already perfect. But Hans resolutely insisted, "No, it is wrong."

After an hour's quarrelling, Hans finally agreed: "Very well, I shall play for you, I shall show you. But then it can never be perfect again and I shall never give another concert on it—I *will* never."

They went to the hall.

There were db-meters everywhere, on the chairs, on the floor, in the aisles, suspended from the ceiling, *überall.* Hans with a great show of reluctance sat himself at the organ, waited for the electronics experts to turn on all their equipment, and then slowly prepared to play. He played the fourth fugue on the inverted subject with another counter-subject, with its characteristic episodes in which Bach uses a leap of a descending third counterpointed with a tetrachord, and the harmonic distortions of the theme. It was surely an adequate test of the perfection of the organ. But Hans was so convinced of the instrument's—yes, *instrument's*—imperfection that he had almost finished the fugue before he realized that the organ was indeed perfect—it was perfect! He leapt to his feet: *"Das ist perfekt, mein Gott, ist das PERFEKT!"*

Hans asked the electronics experts what they had done, and when they insisted they had done nothing, he would have none of it. They had done something, surely, for it was now perfect and before it had not been. Clearly, the electronics experts did not trust Hans's judgment. They quarrelled for a long while until Hans was under one acoustic ceiling and the electronics experts and the manager were under the other. They continued arguing on occasion without suffering any loss in volume from one side of the hall to the other, because after all, the acoustics were very nearly perfect. Finally, Hans was reduced to muttering, "They lie, they all lie," over and over; and the electronics experts and the manager were reduced to collective pouting.

After a perfectly intolerable period of muttering and pouting, one of the electronics experts jumped to his feet. "That's it, that's it!"

Hans yelled back, "What *is* it?" for he never contracted his words, but gave to each its perfectly full value.

The electronics expert was moving chairs and db-meters and oscilloscopes without clarifying the mystery for the benefit of anyone. Then he told the manager and all the other electronics experts to join him on the chairs clustered around the db-meters. But, clearly, he was not satisfied with the arrangement. He asked the manager to fetch other people. The manager left and returned after twenty minutes with the chorus which was to perform that evening. The electronics expert placed all the choralers in a huge cluster around and among the db-meters.

Then he turned to Hans: "Play, Herr Strobel, play."

Though angry, Hans was curious. Hence, he played, if reluctantly.

He played the fifth fugue, a stretto fugue in contrary motion on the main subject and the inversion, in which the two forms of the theme are worked in various canons. At the end of the fugue, as the two forms sounded together, Hans leapt from the stool and declared, "It is wrong, it is no longer perfect, what have you done?"

The electronics expert enjoyed his moment: "It was the *people,* the people in the audience—they were absorbing and distorting the sounds. That is all there is to it, Herr Strobel. The organ is perfect."

At last Hans was quiet. He stared blankly into the absent audience. He could muster no words for them.

Having discovered the source of the imperfection, Hans now had the manager schedule another performance for him. The announcements in the papers read:

HANS STROBEL

THE ART OF FUGUE
J.S. BACH

PUBLIC NOT ADMITTED

BIOGRAPHICAL NOTES

What We Go By is Russell Hardin's first book. Recently, he has completed a first novel, *Perhaps It Was Never the Same.* His short fictions have appeared in New Orleans Review, Minnesota Review, Mississippi Review and Latitudes. Hardin is presently teaching at the University of Pennsylvania in Philadelphia.

Rochelle Bonazzi's cover design and page drawings are created with black tempera on very small scraps of paper. She is also responsible for the Latitudes imprint which will be our imprint hereafter. That particular drawing appeared in Minnesota Review, as did others there, and a separate group in the last Latitudes.

LATITUDES PRESS BOOKS
Edited and Designed
By Robert Bonazzi

This book was cared for by

Millie Vazquez McDaniel
Roger McDaniel
Leslie V. Metts
Linda Scheer
C.W. Truesdale